YOU ANTHEM
Stories and Reflections of Celebration

A Memoir
Tori Franklin

YOU ANTHEM

Stories and Reflections of Celebration

© 2023, Tori Franklin.

Print ISBN: 979-8-35091-748-2
eBook ISBN: 979-8-35091-749-9

This book is dedicated to those who endure and overcome hardships in solitude. To those who battle with depression yet persevere with a smile for the sake of their loved ones. And to all those seeking healing and growth from their struggles.

Foreword

Dr. Mikalei Y. Gordon, M.D.

Tori and I first met over a computer screen in the midst of the Covid-19 pandemic, her sitting at the desk framing her South Carolina bedroom after training and me in my Chicago office where I practice as a psychiatrist. There was so much about that first encounter that was not truly a meeting as we might think of it in the formal sense. Although we were connected for a specific professional cause, Tori and I entered the appointment with little direct intention other than to exchange our stories and to allow the message of this book to shape the next steps. I'd just finished her manuscript the week before, and it felt as if I'd already met her through the stories laid out on the page. Talking to Tori face-to-face felt like picking up where her book left off.

If there is one thing that strikes me about Tori's writing, it is the ease with which she expresses deep emotion, and the grace with which she presents it to the reader in raw form. But Tori did not come by the insights in this book easily. As she tells it, some discoveries came through long hours of reflection, seeking out self-improvement, mindfulness, meditation, and therapy; all pursuits to turn inward and come closer to discovering oneself truly.

This book is intended to inspire the reader to do the same- to consider and discover aspects of who you are, your values, to build self-esteem and find personal meaning in your own story. Sometimes we can find pieces of ourselves in the story of another person. We learn that we are not alone in the challenges we face. We learn that the human experience and every emotion within it is a shared one.

One of the most beautiful intentions for this writing is the desire to help every reader understand when the kind of self-help offered in this book is sufficient and when more intensive help may be needed. Think of the health classes many of us took at some point in our lives that taught us basic first aid. We learned how to clean and bandage a scrape, how to manage a sprain, how to treat an allergic reaction. These techniques are excellent to use in the field to prevent further injury. But, if a more serious injury were to present itself, most of us would agree this person requires emergency intervention.

This is what first aid does. It teaches people how to manage minor injuries and recognize severe ones, so that they can help the person receive the correct level of treatment. What follows below will be a psychological first aid, of sorts. It is a guide to help shed light on what exactly mental health means and how to find the right kind of help when you need it.

A Guide to Psychological First Aid

What is mental health?

Mental health is the emotional and psychological wellbeing that affects a person's thoughts, feelings, and behaviors. There are basic things we can all do to care of our mental wellness, including preventative measures that help keep us healthy. These include things like getting enough sleep, eating a healthy, balanced diet, getting enough exercise, journaling, meditation and other positive ways of coping with stress, having a safe support network, and taking proper care of your physical health.

These strategies can be used to keep a healthy person healthy. When someone has a mental illness, these strategies are not enough on their own. A person with a mental illness often needs other forms of medical treatment to get better.

When to get help:

The list includes some warning symptoms that signal when it may be time to reach out to a mental health professional for the right kind of help.

Thoughts of suicide or self-harm
Persistent low or negative mood
Erratic mood swings
Sleeping more or less than usual
Eating more or less than usual
Poor concentration
Low energy or motivation

Not enjoying your usual interests or hobbies
Feelings of intense guilt
Feelings of worthlessness
Hopelessness
Seeing or hearing things that others around you cannot
Persistent flashbacks, nightmares, or unwanted memories of traumatic events

Who to reach out to for help:

Psychiatrist—a medical doctor specializing in treating mental health conditions by prescribing medications or other forms of therapy/treatment

Psychologist—a mental health professional with an advanced degree in psychology. They are trained to diagnose mental health conditions and provide talk therapy. Generally, they are not able to prescribe medications.

Therapist or Counselor—a mental health professional trained to provide talk therapy. They are not able to prescribe medications

How to get help:

Dial 988 for mental health crisis help or to be connected with resources in your city.

National Alliance on Mental Illness:

Call 800-950-NAMI to talk

Text NAMI to 741741 in a crisis

Nami.org

MentalHealth.gov

Call your insurance carrier to request a list of in network mental health professionals

Preface

It didn't happen overnight. I didn't just wake up one morning and feel an overwhelming amount of love for myself, with confidence oozing from my skin. No, in fact some days I still feel unworthy. Some nights I still think that I am unseen and unimportant. Those feelings go back a very long way.

My trauma started when my dad moved away from me when I was eight. I felt abandoned, and although we have a great relationship now, that feeling of not being able to get close to anyone for fear that they'll leave never quite went away. From there, I got into relationships with boys I knew I couldn't rely on, because that's what I knew; it's what I thought I deserved.

I quickly adopted the thought that my body was the most valuable thing I had to offer anyone. Years down the line, molestation and assault continued to prove to me how unworthy I was of love, from others and more importantly from myself. Then finally, my senior year of college, I was assaulted by a boy I'd loved for years. This shattered me in every way possible.

My spirit was in pieces that I repeatedly used to cut myself down even further. My self-image was dismantled, and I felt like I had no one. I began to fail my classes, and my passion, track and field, suffered. After months of crying myself to sleep I found that the only way I could get them to stop was to listen to one song, called *Hope*. I don't know how I found it; I like to believe it found me.

This idea of hope was sung into my spirit every night, and I realized that I couldn't give up. I couldn't possibly let this be the end of my journey. Alone, in the dark, with dried mascara stained on my pillowcase and snot dripping from my sleeve, I began vlogging how I felt. If no one else cared about how I felt (which wasn't true) I knew that I did.

As I looked back at myself in the video camera, I began to speak to my reflection. I told myself all the things I loved about me. I called out all of my traits that may not be so great but were still worthy of love. I reminded myself of the boundless, immeasurable love that the Divine has for me and my soul. I looked at my tear-filled eyes and I said, "You. Are. Worthy. And I love you." I may not have believed every word I spoke at the time, but that was the night I created the 'Tori Anthem.' And with this book, I aim to help you develop a You Anthem.

What exactly is a 'You Anthem'? To put it simply, it is an oral expression of love and acceptance of yourself. It is a gathering of affirmations and confirmations of your own greatness. This doesn't eliminate or ignore your short-comings. In fact, it acknowledges the things that need refining about you but seeks to see them with a loving and understanding gaze. These pages hold the story of how I created my own personal anthem.

Slowly, the love I felt for myself grew. As it flourished, so did other aspects of my life. I started eating better, choosing who I allowed in my life more wisely, and had life changing success in my career. One year after I graduated from college, I placed second at the indoor USA Track and Field National Championship. Two years after graduation I won the Indoor USA National Championship and three years out, I broke the Outdoor American Record in the women's triple jump. Four years out, I broke the Indoor American Record in the Women's Triple jump and in 2020 I broke it again. It was a shock to the track and field world. "Who is Tori Franklin," they asked. "Where did she come from?"

Prior to creating the 'You Anthem,' I didn't know the answer to these questions myself. I thought I knew, but I understand now more than ever who I truly am and where I come from. I am light. I am love. And I come from the stars. I am born of love, and I have the endless capacity to not only fill up myself, but to send that love to you and to the world. And the best part about this knowledge is knowing that you too are all of these things.

If you've picked up this book, I hope you find parts of it to resonate with your own experience. Maybe you already know or will recognize that you struggle with some of the same challenges around identity and self-worth. What can the process of healing look like?

How many of us take the time to sit and unravel our issues one by one? How many of us put on our ripped jeans, get on our hands and knees and claw with our fingers in the dirt, grime under our nails, ripping up the roots of our issues, pulling up the weeds and burning them?

It can be terrifying. Who knows what vermin you'll find down there? Or maybe you do know and that's its own sort of fear. Our happiness can never be whole while it is suffocated by weeds.

But you are loved and you are not alone. There are people who will get on their hands and knees, mud on their face, hand rake in tow, and dig up those roots with you. They will dig with you. Trust in those who love you.

Writing this now brings me to tears because I know how hard this journey has been for me. Each anthem is written as a stage in the process of growth. At the end of some anthems, you are directed to where you can find a *challenge* that can aid in your healing. I hope you find parts of it to foster your own growth.

Anyway,

I Love You,
Mee

Acknowledgments

This book owes its existence to the unwavering support of two incredible individuals. Joy Tutela, a kind, passionate, and inspiring literary agent, who wholeheartedly believed in the significance of sharing this story. She read the early drafts when I first began writing in February 2020, and her encouragement shaped the initial part of this memoir. I am profoundly grateful to her.

Colin Diment has been my trusted writing accountability partner for many years. We exchanged writings, edited each other's work, often revisiting them two or three times. Colin has witnessed the evolution and improvement of my writing, and I credit him significantly for that growth. His thought-provoking questions pushed me to expand my words, and I cannot thank him enough.

I am forever indebted to my grandmother, Demerette Kee, for instilling in me a deep love for words and reading. Her influence in my early years helped me discover the power of conveying emotions through words and the lasting impact they can have on someone's life.

I thank my mother for continuously nurturing my passion for writing. She has bought me countless journals for as long as I can remember. What started as youthful babble about boys has matured into a profound means of expressing life's complexities. Without her subtle nudges to document it all, I wouldn't have developed and honed this talent.

Thank you to the young and talented Alexandra Yaneva for the amazing book cover and internal illustrations. Her passion to create, willingness to learn, and overall enthusiasm about the project made working with her so much fun and exciting.

Dr. Mikalei Y. Gordon, M.D. for the beautiful forward and encouragement. I am grateful to my therapist, Kissala Mouyabi, for his guidance in my personal growth and for helping me maintain my sanity. I am deeply appreciative of my dad, friends, brothers, and sisters for the love and the life that they infuse into me.

Lastly, I'd like to thank those that have supported me on this journey. Whether I know you personally or not your support and well wishes continue to help me push forward.

The contents of this book are written and recalled to the best of my memory. The true names that are shared have given their consent to be used and others are changed for their privacy.

Contents

Part One

Who Am I?

Anthem —
(noun) a song of praise or devotion; a sacred vocal song.

An anthem is a dance that you do in the privacy of your room or on a crowded dance floor, evoking a sense of freedom. It is a poem written from the soul, spilling the truth of your spirit in deep black ink. It is a song sung in the shower. A hug given. A kiss received. An anthem is a meditation of gratitude, a prayer of love. It is an affirmation of all that encompasses you.

Anthem 1

I've noticed that I rarely, if ever, write or talk about track and field. Which I find to be intriguing in a way. I've been doing it for twelve and a half years. I actually had to stop and count the years on my fingers. Why not talk about something I do for a living? The one thing that gives me purpose. I've always tried to separate myself from it. I'm not only an athlete or track star. I like to dance and sing, listen to poetry, and I enjoy thriller films. I attempt to play the violin and I give public speeches on occasion.

Maybe it's because the world of track and field is scary, so unforgiving and forgetful. You can be amazing one day and come dead last the next. You could win all the awards this year, but next year be forgotten. Or maybe, it's because this truly is who I am, an athlete. I love being an athlete, and it's scary to be so passionate about something that you won't get to pursue forever. When you are old or broken or simply not good enough anymore, that's it. There is no 'good job', 'you were great in your years with us.' Track won't miss you. It will forget you the moment you unlace your spikes. Your name is likely to never be mentioned again.

It's hard to love something or someone so much. I guess I do my best not to get too attached.

Jumping gives me a reason… a reason to not eat cupcakes every day, a reason to attempt to be mentally fit. When I'm competing on the runway or running around an empty track at night, I'm at peace. I'm just so unapologetically, so effortlessly, happy. I feel alive. I feel important.

There's this adrenaline, all eyes on me. I have the power to conduct thousands of people to clap rhythmically as one, all for me. All of them wanting to see me do something amazing. One breath to center myself, refocus, and I'm off. I barely remember running down the runway. My eyes don't see it, but my body feels it. Each phase, smooth, gliding, wind, then I'm stretching my legs for the edge of the pit, tossing sand everywhere. Before I even stand the crowd erupts. This energy is incredible. When you succeed on such a grand scale, it makes all the fear worth it. Whether they know my name or not, these moments will be mine forever.

Anthem 2

Who Am I Really?

November 3, 2016

Why is it that if I'm alone for an extended number of hours, not busied by television or my hair or some other activity that I've cooked up, I tend to lose myself to my mind. To the dark corners of it. Those thoughts that I have, the bashing and self-hatred, is that normal? The lingering thoughts on everything that has ever hurt me, does that happen to others? I get so sad and I wonder, is this who I really am? Is THIS me? Is all the smiling and goofiness a façade, a cruel joke upon myself, pretending that I am happy? And when all is said and done, when the friends are away and work is finished, the day is through and all that is left is you and your mind...is that the real me?

"There comes a time, somewhere in the middle of every woman's life, when Mother Nature herself stands behind us and wraps her arms around our shoulders, whispering, "its time. You have taken enough now. It's time to stop growing up, stop growing older and start growing wiser—and wilder."

– Donna Ashworth

Anthem 3

When I am in the thick of it, when the anxiety has a hold on my neck and sadness has wrapped its cold and murky arms around my body, when the only thoughts that make it through are the ones constantly putting me down, it feels impossible to catch a break. The storm rages in my mind, chucking debris into my eyes and I am left cowering in the fetal position, blinded by my own self-doubt, self-loathing, and self-pity. I know how this happens. It starts with one thought, then another on top, then one worse, then the one that really hurts. The thoughts that shoot an arrow straight to my core, where only I know that pain exists.

Your mind can be your worst enemy. You know everything about you. Every heartbreak, every snide comment that made you feel terrible about yourself, every failure that you haven't quite gotten over. Your mind could CUT YOU DOWN. And I know all about it. I've spent nights crying about how worthless I felt. I've been in Germany at a track meet trying to stop the tears from erupting because I didn't have confidence in myself that day. I've cried the whole way home after having sex with a boy I loved because I felt used and unworthy. Each of these moments started with a thought.

Every thought you have shapes your reality. When you think badly about yourself or a situation, you project that negative energy onto yourself and that situation. It is the energy that you put out into the world that you will receive from it. Your thoughts have immense power. Every positive thought you have negates a negative. Every positive thought you put out aids in creating a world that benefits you and your wellbeing.

In the year leading up to the 2021 Olympics, I went through an immense mental transition. Every time I competed in college and in my early years as a professional, I built up this animalistic aggression that I felt like I needed to jump well. If it was present naturally, I'd do really well, like the time I broke the outdoor American Record. Other times, the jittery anger wasn't there, and I'd try to force it. I listened to my "Pumped Up Kix" playlist and jumped around until my heart was running rampant. I gulped espresso and talked shit to imaginary competitors. "*These b*#ches ain't ready!!*" Ultimately, it was exhausting. I became tired before the competition was over and my technique was sloppy.

I later noticed that the aggressive nature of my competitiveness was present less and less. I thought this meant I was losing my edge, and that's why I felt the need to create that artificial energy. Weeks before the Olympic Trials, I sat and meditated. A voice whispered to me, "*let it go.*" I don't need to hold on to who I was before the 2020 Pandemic. She was great, she carried us this far in our career, but it's time to let her go. I am evolving. From that moment, I stopped trying to be who I was and I learned to accept who I am *now*.

As the trials got closer, I meditated more and more. I practiced imagery, the act of imagining the competition… from the smell of the grass, to the sound of the crowd, to my run and jumps on the runway. I changed the music that I listened to; It became more peaceful, spiritual music that made me feel alive, loved, and happy. And when I was on the field at the 2021 Olympic Trials, I harnessed a new energy. It wasn't based in aggression; it was based in love and power. I jumped the farthest I'd jumped all season and qualified for my first Olympic Team to Tokyo, Japan.

I used meditation to alter my mindset so that I could compete efficiently. Meditation is the act of bringing stillness to your mind and allowing you simply to "be" in the moment exactly as you are. I changed my power source from a negative based energy (anger) to positive based energy (love). Functioning from a place of peace gave me more of an edge and wasted less of my energy.

Be present challenge is found on page 47

Anthem 4

I read a book called, 'Why Meditate,' written by many different authors and edited by Clint Willis. It talks about how meditation aids in various aspects of our lives.

There's a passage that I believe explains 'anger' and ultimately how to relate to and address it. "Most contemporary psychological research shows that when one expresses anger quite often in one's life, it leads to the easy expression of anger. Expressing anger becomes a habit. Many people assume that we have a certain amount of anger inside, and that if we do not want to keep it inside, we have to put it outside; somehow if it is outside, it is not going to be inside anymore. Anger seems like a solid thing. But, in fact, we discover, if we observe carefully, that anger has no solidity. In reality, it is merely a conditioned response that arises and passes away. It is crucial for us to see that when we identify with these passing states as being solid and who we truly are, we let them rule us, and we are compelled to act in ways that cause harm to ourselves and others. Anger is an emotion with a lot of different components. There are strands of disappointment, fear, and sadness all woven together. If the emotions and thoughts are taken as a whole, anger appears as one solid thing. But, if we were to break it down and see its various aspects, we can see the ultimate nature of this experience. We can see that anger is impermanent and it arises and passes away like a wave that comes and goes. We can see that anger is unsatisfactory; it does not bring us joy. It does not rise according to our will, or whim, or wish. It arises when conditions are right for it to arise. We can see that it is not ours;

we do not own it, we do not possess it. We cannot control anger's rising, we can only relate to it in a skilled way."

Reading this reminds me of all the times when I'm alone and sadness comes, and I begin to wonder if that is the "real me," when I wonder if the joyous, funny, excitable me is just for show. I was beginning to let temporary emotions define me. I was identifying in the low moments. I know now that that isn't who I am. I was low for a period of time due to circumstances. But I will not allow my transient emotions to cause me to believe something bad about myself or make me feel insecure about who I am. Those moments don't define me. Anger does not define me. In truth, neither does the joy I also often feel. I AM NOT the emotions I feel.

Anthem 5

Nature's Embrace

November 7, 2020

I hugged a tree today
Cuz no one hugs me
It's been weeks since another
has touched my body
Not for sex, not in play, not for intimacy
Not a soul was around
So I hugged a tree

Anthem 6

My childhood experiences coupled with my experiences of assault left me feeling like my body is anything but sacred. In my mind, my body was unfit to give to a proper lover. Because of this mindset, I didn't care much for my body or what happened to it. I could shut my mind off and let it be taken advantage of. When I was young this is what I learned was important. This is what I realized was the only thing of worth about me... my body.

With all it's been through, and the actions I took in my attempt to reclaim my body, it left me feeling like it's too damaged. Too damaged to give to someone I love and have a genuine connection with. To me, my body was 'shame' itself, and whenever I got into a relationship it was sex that tended to be difficult for me. The thought alone of giving myself to an amazing person who I love and who loves me, terrified me. I imagined opening myself up to him, sharing my body's secrets and him turning me away. But everyone's body has bones, and everyone's bones have secrets.

My aunt was really self-conscious of her skin when she was in high school; her face was riddled with acne and it made her feel less beautiful. My friend Tay hated when classmates made fun of the size of his lips. Another friend, Alia, always compared her body to the other women around her. One minute she thought she was too big and the next she thought her butt wasn't big enough. Emmanuel felt like his "soft" body wasn't attractive or masculine enough. I have large feet. When I was younger, with twigs for legs, my feet shot out from beneath me like two paddle boats.

Feeling beautiful and worthy in your skin is hard. It is HARD. Social media and beauty propaganda shove these images of thin waist, thick hips, plump lips, and perfect skin in our faces. We see strong chested, buff armed, full bearded men with every swipe. Cheek lifts, lip plumpers, nose jobs, steroids, hair plugs, and contouring are apparently the go-to if you're dissatisfied with any part of your body. Why wouldn't you do it too if you see all the attention these people get when they do? How could you not feel a little self-conscious about your round nose or pear shape in a world like this… a world where every woman is sexualized but reprimanded for being sexual. Where every man is forced to feel like they *have to* want sex all the time from whoever is willing to give it.

Our bodies may not be perfect according to the mainstream standards of beauty propaganda, but they are perfect in their imperfection. Our bodies are made as they are for us specifically. They are the vessels for our souls to roam the Earth in this magnificent human experience. This body was *given* to *YOU*. If you can give love to it, take care of it, and be good to it, it will stay healthy and be good to you. We need our bodies to navigate this world, and we must take care of it like if it were a child; wash it, feed it healthy options, exercise it, prep it for events.

It is a gift to be here and now in this form, so take advantage of this. A healthy body cultivates a healthy mind and a healthy mind nourishes a peaceful spirit. When you find love and confidence in your body, other people notice and they too see the beauty in your body as well.

*Loving Gaze Challenge found on page 50**

Anthem 7

Nate's One-Liners

November 2016

I'm honestly tired of writing about Nate, but I hear his voice in my head all the time, just his one liners. The little things he has said in passing, sometimes over a year ago. This morning I was getting dressed and I looked into the mirror at the reflection of my legs, "Powerful," ran across my mind. When I would change in front of him, lying in my bed only made for one person, he would sit up, grab my thighs and say, "Powerful," then lay back down.

The other day, I was riding my bike to work. The sun was particularly bright this day. I closed my eyes just for a moment and tilted my head up towards the sun, letting the warmth circulate through my body. I flashed back to when he and I were lying in the sheets during the winter. A sliver of sunlight shone through my curtains and warmed our bodies the same way. Nate put his hands around my face, peering into my soul and whispered, "You are the goddamn Light." He was the first person to ever say that to me. I've believed it ever since... not because he said it, but because I know it's the truth. I wish I had said it back to him. Even if we know it's true, we may often need to be reminded. So, I hope that he knows he's the goddamn Light too.

Anthem 8

I do wonder, if I hadn't been through trauma, what would my mindset be? What kind of person would I be now? Would I be as resilient or more resilient? Would I be more or less able to motivate and inspire through my experiences? I wonder whether the mindset or the trauma came first.

Sometimes it feels like people are judging my trauma, comparing, ranking, analyzing it to justify how they think I should be reacting. I somehow receive the message that anything shy of rape should be grieved less. How much emotional pain should I be feeling? It seems like it is measured for me in the responses I get from those I confide in.

I've had three separate people challenge my experience. Each one responded with, "but there was no intercourse," or "so he didn't rape you?" I want to scream so they understand, "assault is illegal too!" but I can't find my voice in the moment. Some days I just feel angry that I don't have a tangible reason that makes sense to everyone why I felt so betrayed that night. Then the next person won't have to say, "I don't mean to demean what happened to you, I'm just trying to understand why you were upset?" When tears well up in my eyes as I tell the story, they'll know exactly why.

Many times, during my adolescent life I was fondled, grabbed, touched inappropriately, and told to do things by teens older than me, both boy and girl. I didn't know it was something I could stop. It happened so much with multiple people that it became normal to me. I really thought this was routinely happening to other little girls too.

M.P never knew about my childhood, but he knew enough about me. He meant something to me and through our eight years together, I thought I meant something to him too. His actions confused me, hurt me. Why would he put his hands on me when I continually asked him not to? I was in tears and he wouldn't stop. He was supposed to love me and respect me. Yet, here he was doing what all those other kids had done so many years before, and I wanted to kill him for it.

Shame is something I am still slowly shedding. It clings to me, gripping at my elbows, and shackling me from my feet as I try to break free. Shame. It's like a weighted blanket, if the blanket carried the weight of mountains. And every time you try to dig your nails into the ground to pull yourself from beneath, it grabs you by the chin, stares you in the face and says, "Look at it! Look at you! Look at what you did! Look at what happened to you! You should be ashamed. You. Should. Be. Ashamed." Shame is attached to every past action we wish we would've done differently. It's melded to the thoughts you wish you don't have; the feelings you wish you didn't feel. It's joined with the experiences we believe make us awful, unlovable human beings. With guilt comes shame. And with shame, comes regret.

At a very young age, I experienced various forms of sexual abuse. Older boys throwing their heavy bodies on top of mine, forcing me to look at them or touch them. Older girls asking me to undress and do things no child should. For years it left me confused about my sexual identity. I didn't know if my experiences with those girls "made me lesbian". I didn't know if I was dirty or if I was considered 'sexually promiscuous'. I didn't know if my body's natural reaction to it meant that I liked it and that I was an active participant. Meaning, there was no one to blame but myself. And for all of this, I was ashamed.

Years of bad dating decisions piled on that shame until my self-worth was null. I thought myself to be equal to the lowest of animals. When I was sexually harassed in college it merely reconfirmed my entire mental perception of myself. I am solely valuable in terms of sexual acts.

Guilt. Shame. Regret.

In the novel, *Aleph,* by Paolo Coelho, there's a passage about a young woman who explains her sexual abuse as a child to a dinner table full of strangers. The character, Hilal, was abused by a neighbor, the father of one of her friends. He'd touch her and ask her to touch him. She said the worst part about her abuse was that she started to enjoy it, even though she knew it was wrong. Coelho went on to write, "And because I carried all that guilt around inside me, because victims always end up considering themselves to be culprits, I decided to keep punishing myself. So, in my relationships with men, I've always sought suffering, conflict, and despair."

I'd never read or seen a victim of child sexual abuse admit this. It's exactly what has kept shame lingering inside of me. I always felt that if I liked it then it wasn't abuse. If I liked it then I must be some kind of disgusting harlot. It's the reason I've kept the abuse quiet for so many years or only discussed it lightheartedly and casually. I've never admitted anything like that to anyone. I've never even written it before. To admit that your body took pleasure in the act (…look at me saying "your". Disconnecting myself from the conversation, as if it were no longer me who feels this way).

It is me.

Some of it felt nice. Some of it was exciting in a way. But all of it was wrong. I was too young for all of it and it should have never happened.

I don't feel any less shameful, but acknowledgment is the first step…or so they say. I had to learn that it wasn't my fault. I was too young to choose to do anything. I was not unlovable in any way. We all make mistakes. We all have done things we wish we didn't, or experienced stuff we wished we hadn't. None of it dictates your worth. None of it defines your being. You don't need to feel ashamed, guilty, and regretful. You are not the same person you were when all this happened to you or when you made those decisions. You have evolved.

Anthem 9

Worthy

March 2, 2020

There's something that doesn't quite connect. When I tell myself "I am worthy," there's a part of me that obviously isn't believing this. There's a voice within me screaming, "I call bullshit!" I turn to look at it, then look away, like, well I tried. And I leave it over there sitting in its dark corner, smoking a cigar, with a French beret on like a heckler at a poetry slam.

When I say I am worthy, who am I talking to? Who is listening? Who is it that I'm trying to reach?

Of course, I believe I'm worthy when the sun is shining on my face and I am full of life and happiness, almost manically. But what part of me really needs to hear this?

Is it the me I am now, sitting on this train, present and contemplating the thought? Is it the me during my childhood assaults? The me who broke the American Record and was on top of the world? Or the me that was looked at like a savage rodent in college after spilling my soul to a boy. Is it me after my ex, M.P choked me in the car, the me taken advantage of while intoxicated, the me who gives public speeches on mental health to kids or the me that cries in bed contemplating the many ways I could end it all? And is she listening? When I speak these words of affirmation, is she listening?

Am I going deep enough so that she can hear me or am I sitting at the dock of my consciousness looking down at the deep blue waters and hoping she can hear me thousands of miles below? And if she could, would she believe me?

I want to know how to build my worth. Simply reciting the words, merely dipping my toes into the water doesn't touch on anything. It won't work if not all of me is listening and not all of me believes it. So how do I get her to listen?

Anthem 10

I'm on the precipice of sliding, no, falling into an anxiety-ridden depression. It creeps up on me like storm clouds in the distance. It waits until my next weak moment, and I begin to hear the drops of rain all around me. I dodge it with distractions but eventually, inevitably, the clouds are pouring above me. Soaked in my insecurities and fear.

Last night I sobbed until my stomach ached and my head throbbed. I was drunk on wine and wondered whether wine and Tylenol would make it all stop.

"Something is wrong with me" I repeated. "I can't do this."

I cried until I slept, woke up the next morning and cried some more.

I recited the Tori Anthem, over and over. It worked for a few hours. It allowed me to get up and have lunch.

I haven't meditated in three weeks. The darkness in me wants me to be miserable. It wants me to blow things up. It wants me to feel alone. It wants me to identify with it. It wants me to think I AM misery, that I AM depression and sadness and guilt and shame. That these are in my DNA, but they aren't. I AM NOT these things.

I AM LIGHT. I AM LOVE. I AM WORTHY.

Reflecting on a low point journal challenge found on page 53

Anthem 11

I had a hard time starting this entry, but somehow in my thought process I remembered a question my teammate once asked me. She asked, "Have you always had this positive mindset? Have you always just had this happy mentality?" I hesitated before answering. I wasn't sure what to say. So I said, "Yes…well for a long time at least."

I thought deeper on what caused this hesitation and why "yes," isn't the full truth. I wasn't a particularly happy and bubbly child growing up. Not like the kids on social media who just giggle for no reason. I wasn't super social or extra positive when I was young. Choosing optimism as I aged was a response to sexual abuse and the emotional instability, I often felt within me. I recognized early on that I felt deeply. I had bouts of angry outburst from elementary school through high school. Fighting, bullying, and just getting into mischief. There were periods when I was so angry, my blood boiled inside me just waiting to explode. But I couldn't let anyone see that side of me, I liked the perception of being the goofy, fun, good girl that my mother and others saw when they looked at me. I knew I couldn't survive on the anger, sadness, and shame that I hid. I wouldn't have been able to live with it. This happiness became a defense mechanism, a survival tactic, so that I could withstand each day.

As I thought through this, I burst into tears. I cried for my younger self that had to go through all that she did and for feeling like she had to create this survival tactic. I cried as a grown woman for a child who has suffered, just as I would cry if I'd heard the story happening to any other child. It's terrible, and no child should have to experience that or feel how I felt about myself for decades after.

All of my experiences have made me who I am. And this tactic of happiness and positivity has turned into a genuine lifestyle. I'm grateful for that. I'm proud of little me for getting us here, for helping us survive. But I don't need to be in survival mode anymore. I am safe now. I can take care of my emotional needs. I don't have to hide who I am or what I feel. If I feel sad I will feel it. If anger arises within me, I will allow it to express itself and then I will let it go. I am free to express what I feel and know that I am still loved. I can express emotions and know that I am still LOVE.

Anthem 12

I looked up a therapist yesterday. I think I need more help than I can do by myself.

I need help.

I searched for one on this French doctor app they have here. I found an older man, late forties. I was on my way to the dentist and I just wanted to save the number, so I called then immediately hung up. Whether or not I would've ended up calling him again I don't know, but I didn't need to. He called me back ten minutes later.

I told him I called on accident, and he said that it was okay and asked if now was a good time for a quick talk. He asked how I found his number and I told him, and then I said that I'd been having a difficult time and needed to talk to someone.

We scheduled a session for later that day.

It went well. He was kind, welcoming, and wanted me to feel safe. We talked about a lot of stuff, and he's got a pretty good understanding of a few of my traumas. It was both an exciting and scary interaction. Exciting, because I found a therapist that I can (hopefully) feel comfortable with. Scary, because the thought of the healing process sounds awful. But I'm up for it. I'm tired of hurting.

Anthem 13

I had another therapy session this afternoon. I told my therapist about my childhood experiences. I mentioned Porsha, who would sit on top of me bare-bodied when we slept over at the baby-sitter's house. He asked me how little me felt in those moments, and I couldn't give him a clear answer. I'd shrug my shoulders and say, "I don't know, sad?" He talked me into doing a guided meditation/ visualization to try to connect with my younger self.

I closed my eyes as he coached me deep into my root chakra. The darkness engulfed me. Huddled in the empty void was a small child crying softly into herself. I approached her cautiously. I reached out to her and she'd shudder. I could feel her without speaking.

"How does she feel?" he asked.
"She's afraid to speak."
"Afraid of what?"
I paused, knowing the answer but afraid myself to even say it.

"She's afraid of judgement. She's ashamed…. for not *saying* no. She didn't feel like she had a choice, but by not saying no she thinks that made her an active participant."

Mr. K. reassured her that he was not here to judge her. He told her that she is safe here. We asked "little me" what she needed from us. She whimpered, "Understanding," from him and that she wanted me to protect her, to keep her safe.

Tears slipped their way through my eyelids and flowed down my cheeks. He had me wrap my arms around myself and tell her that I have learned now. I am capable of taking care of her and protecting her now. I know how and when to say no. She cried with me as her tension released.

I looked around at the cold dark space that I'd found her in. This was no place for this piece of me to live. I created a home for her. Where there was once nothing, I imagined a vast field of bright green grass. There was a garden with thriving, colorful fruits and vegetables. Tall trees with plenty of branches to climb sprouted from the Earth. Birds, rabbits, and sunlight filled the space. I imagined a long, broad table with piles of all her favorite food. Fruit plates of papaya, apples, grapes, and dragon fruit, veggie plates full of squash, sweet potatoes, okra, and zucchini. Fresh made macaroni and cheese, cupcake towers, water, lemonade, Twizzlers, and herbs scattered about it all.

I watched her eyes light up when she saw the sun and big blue sky. She looked at me and smiled. I told her we can talk whenever she wants. I kneeled beside her and said, "You are safe."

The darkness, shame, and fear were hidden away into a box. I dug it a 30-foot hole in the ground and locked it away far from where it could ever find her. Her garden was a safe space.

I opened my eyes and the remaining tears slid to my chin. I smiled and took a breath that filled my entire body.

"We need to do this with each part of you. Each trauma, at each age, because they need different things."

I nodded and thanked him.

Anthem 14

I ran myself a bath this afternoon. Warm, but not so hot that I'd start sweating in the water. I drizzled chamomile bubble bath solution into the running faucet. I poured pink Epsom salt into the water and watched the water glow a soft rose hue. My laptop was nearby playing Raveena's Lucid album. I soaked and listened to the entire thing and replayed a few of the songs at the end.

I lay with my eyes closed until I began to wash. I grabbed the scrub that is used to remove dead skin. I scrubbed from my feet up my entire body. I scrubbed my legs, thinking of all the men/women who touched them without permission and I rubbed them away. I scrubbed my thighs, removing the shame of my sexuality, of my childhood abuse, and of sex in general. I scrubbed my chest, releasing the dead cells of heartbreak and heartache. I cleaned my back of all the sweaty, anxiety-ridden nights. I washed my neck, removing the residue of tears.

Then I sat. I sat in the water of my muck, my regrets, my shame, my unworthiness. I sat clean and refreshed, surrounded by it all, and then I closed my eyes to meditate. I breathed. I told myself to let it go as the same songs replayed themselves. I told myself it's okay to let it go. I felt something rise from my root, up through my stomach to my chest, and then to my neck, where it got stuck

"It's okay," I said.
"I love you."
I started panting. Tears rose to my eyes.
"I do. I love you so much." Water began to flow.

"I love you to the moon and back. I know you don't think you're worthy of love or that you can love others, but you are and you can. You are worthy. God loves you. I love you. You are loved." The blockage in my throat released as I sobbed softly into the bath of my discarded soot. I cried. I breathed. I loved.

When my breathing calmed, I stood up, emptied the tub, and ran the shower to clean any leftovers off of my body.

I'm outside now. Writing in the grass. Sun on my skin. Feeling. Being.

Anthem 15

Regaining Control
January 11, 2017

You'd be surprised at how comforting a teddy bear can be. I bought Leo two years ago when I felt like I had no one to talk to. No comfort, no safety. M.P, the man who brought the anger, took those things from me when he put his hands on me. But Leo, he listens so well. He holds me and lets my tears become his.

Sometimes I have days when I know the evening will be hard, when I'll weep for no reason. I do everything I can to make plans, so I won't be alone. It doesn't always help, but it lessens the darkness at least until I get home where I'm once again on my own. Like I said, it doesn't always help.

Out of nowhere my eyes are flooded, I collapse where I stand. Even as I cry, I try to whisper, "I love you, I love you Tori, I love you." I know I should believe it, but it's hard to fix a problem when I don't know what it is. The tears just keep rolling. I've lost control. I've lost control. If only I knew how much I am loved, if only I knew how grand I am, if only I believed all the great things that others have told me, maybe I wouldn't feel so hopeless. Maybe I wouldn't be laying on this old dirty carpet. So alone.

I know it's crazy to still carry around this bear. I recognize that he is only a physical representation of the comfort that I need to find within myself. I listen to me so well. I hold space for myself to feel. I remind myself of my love energy.

Finally, I get through the static of my own mess. I hear it. "I love you," I tell myself. "I love you," I say again like a whisper come from above me. My breathing slows, my eyes dry. I whisper, "sleep" and I comply.

"Only someone who can say 'I love you' is
capable of saying 'I forgive you'"

– Aleph Paulo Coelho

*Moving through emotions meditation is found on page 56**

Anthem 16

I love to live my life as freely as possible, as openly as possible, and as genuinely as possible. Living my life free of expectation and pressure, whether from myself or others, allows me to live more in the moment.

One thing I always ask people is, "What brings you true joy?" "What makes you feel most free?" Many people are confused by the question. Joy? Free? Uh...video games, they say. Or they simply have no idea They haven't taken the time to get in touch with their truest self to see what brings their soul complete and utter contentment.

For me, it's dancing. Not because I am a great dancer or because I have some deep understanding and appreciation for music. It's because I allow myself to let go of any inhibitions or fears of judgement and just be in that moment. It doesn't matter what type of music it is... I listen to the beat, feel the rhythm, and glide through the sound waves. Often, I close my eyes and enter into my own world, swaying my body gently or jumping with my arms wild.

Finding something that allows you to 'be' your freest self is a key element in learning to love yourself and live a freer life. It could be writing, singing, making music, playing a sport, distance running, drawing, yoga, reading a great book, or hiking. It could be watching the ocean waves, feeling the sun on your skin, counting stars, biking down a hill and feeling the wind on your face. Whatever it is that helps you feel bliss, openness, and childlike joy.

Think about the last time you felt this way. Where were you? Who were you with? What were you doing? Whatever comes to mind, notice what brings happiness to the child within you.

Finding something that brings you happiness, even for a moment, brings more happiness into your life overall. And that's the goal, isn't it? To rid ourselves of the passing clouds of sadness and self-loathing and to find a way to love ourselves and enjoy life.

When you do something that you love, do you ever notice how nothing else matters in that moment. Nothing else has your attention except that feeling of joy. We are fully present. This is an easy and fun way to practice presence.

Take a moment to look up from this page. RIGHT NOW! LOOK UP! Notice who or what is around you. Feel the space you're in. You are in the NOW. When you're in the moment, you are not thinking about tasks you need to accomplish or scenarios you might find yourself in. You are in that room, on that train, in that bed, on that toilet, at that desk. Wherever you are, BE THERE!

Often, in darkness, we are not paying attention to the moment at hand. We are lost in our heads… stuck somewhere in the past, somewhere in the future, or somewhere under the covers spewing venom at our bones. We stop noticing what life is offering us at the very moment. And it's just that, LIFE.

You are here, which means you have a chance to experience happiness, love, adventure, and growth. Bring that child-like joy and curiosity into your everyday life. Learn to be aware and content with the Now, however it presents itself to you. Believe me it won't always be a pleasant now, but if you stop to accept this present moment, then you can let life do what it does. It's often our minds that make events more negative than they need to be.

Anthem 17

One of my friends who I've known since high school, Chris, was living in Thailand for three years. He left without having any idea what he was going to do there or how he'd get by financially. There was a period of time when he was living on the streets, was quickly running out of money, and had no idea what he'd do next. As he stood on the street corner contemplating which way to walk, a couple on a moped stopped at the light and pointed their finger at him. "You!"

They sensed his positive and loving energy and invited him into their home. Since then, he has been learning the art of energy healing and the many wisdoms of Dharma. He's been a guiding light in my life when I've needed it most. He's always had a way of messaging me right when I need him to.

In 2019, I was preparing for the World Championship meet. I didn't feel prepared. I wasn't confident in my abilities and I was on the edge of breaking down. In the midst of my mental crisis Chris texted me, "Expectation is the beginning of suffering. Release the expectation and life will fall into place…Flowers and butterflies and sunshine and all. That's Buddha through me."

I felt a weight lift from my shoulders. The dread that was following me around was that of expectation. It was the pressure of having to perform. I was able to breathe.

I still didn't do as well as I'd hoped to at that meet, but it wasn't the end of the world. It became a moment to learn from and ultimately pushed me into a new life adventure living abroad in Paris, France.

It's not simply the act of having expectations that is so crippling. It's being attached to them when life turns out differently. When we expect certain things from people or expect situations to go a certain way and they don't, it reinforces our already preconceived opinions of ourselves.

Maybe a relationship that you expected to last ends. What does your mind do next? Does it make up reasons why, saying things like "it's because I'm too much to handle. I'm too clingy. I'm too weird." Or maybe not getting a job you wanted (or into the university you applied for) turns into "I'm incompetent. I wouldn't be able to do it well anyways. I'm not smart enough."

When life gives us something other than what we expect and our minds struggle to make sense of it, the resulting thoughts are what spiral us back into a depression. But when we learn to be in the moment as it is, accept life EXACTLY as it is, and not hold tightly to our expectations of it, we can navigate life more tactfully. And in the end, enjoy life more fully.

Anthem 18

I went on a solo trip to the south of France. I stayed just outside of Marseille, in a small town called Le Rove. It had one grocery store and two weaving roads. The morning after I arrived, I set out to find a particularly beautiful beach I'd heard about. I got on a bike with gears that clicked with every turn and a seat that rotated while I pedaled. I rode up and down mountainous hills, sometimes riding the same roads twice because I'm directionally challenged.

After an hour and a half of sweating, with my quads burning from the exertion, I had to hike along the side of a mountain. I looked down at the drop straight to the raging waves; it was both terrifying and invigorating. When I finally arrived at the beach I had been pursuing, I took pictures, posted some videos to social media, and then sat down.

The first thoughts I had were, *I should leave by four, the sun will be setting behind the mountains. I'll probably shower really quick then make what I had for dinner last night again. Maybe I'll get some writing done or watch a show.*

I'd spent two hours trying to get to this beautiful beach with a view of the city of Marseilles. The sun was shining, and the water was perfectly blue. But where was I? Lost in my mind, thinking about what I was going to do next instead of being present at this beach that I had worked so hard to get to.

How can I live one moment at a time? I want to focus on one really intentional thing at a time. I want to be present each day. From the moment I wake up, presence, and being aware of everything I am doing or feeling. I try to focus on every sensation and fully experience it mentally, physically, and spiritually. I remind myself *I am here* all throughout the day.

Anthem 19

While My Heart Beats
December 30 2016

Have you ever just been sitting still, eyes wide, not focused on anything, and realize that you aren't still at all. Your entire body is moving slightly. With every beat of your heart your body rocks gently forward. I look at my hands and I can feel the blood rushing through my veins, feeding oxygen to all crevices of my body.

Have you ever been lying on your stomach, ear to the mattress, and notice the sound of your own heartbeat? The sound used to scare me. I feared I would one day hear it stop. Just silence, and then it'd all be over. My life would end right there.

I'm not frightened anymore. In fact, I like these moments, noticing that I'm alive, that my heart is beating, that the fight isn't over. There is still so much to do while my heart beats. No moment to waste. Making moves, improving on my character, opening new pockets of my mind. I have to find a way to make this life worthwhile. To make this life mean something, while my heart beats.

"The present moment is filled with joy and happiness. If you are attentive, you will see it."

– Thich Nhat Hanh

Anthem 20

I went to the beach and played all on my own. I let my imagination bloom and explore faraway lands and mystical creatures. I built castles out of sand and pretended that the people of the village were in a rush to build a moat before the next wave came crashing into their homes. Every time the tide came in, I yelled and squealed as if tiny people were being flooded and ravaged by fifty-foot waves. They were never able to build a moat fast enough.

The land was eventually over run with finger dinosaurs. My index and ring finger the front legs, my thumb and pinky finger the hind legs and my middle finger protruding forward like the long neck dinosaur, the Brachiosaurus. I made loud moaning noises that I imagine dinosaurs must have made as they reshaped this historic castle into a home for themselves.

I could sense onlookers staring at me, a twenty-eight-year-old woman playing in the sand with her fingers and squealing to herself. I know I looked crazy, but it was really fun. I was allowing myself to be silly, to be imaginative, to be a child again. Sometimes I'd try to hum and casually lower my voice when someone caught me by surprise by walking past me. It was an awful attempt at looking "normal".

But you never see young children hide their imagination. It's something we are taught to quiet as we age. What if we gave ourselves permission, at any age, to be goofy, make weird sounds, and play with finger dinosaurs? How joyous life would be.

Anthem 21

> ### A Change in the Wind
> *April 12, 2017*
>
> I feel like a lot of things are changing within me. The more I read, the more I reflect and meditate, the more I feel myself remolding. I'm not sure how exactly, but I'm beginning to feel different.
>
> I can't try to force myself to be who I "expect" myself to be. Not only are we as people influenced by societal norms or expectations of those around us, but we are also shaped by the expectations we place on ourselves. Sometimes this is good. It helps us to push forward, motivates us to succeed. But what if those expectations don't fit with what you NEED or who YOU are. It's so confusing, because part of me always saw myself being a boss of some grand company or owning my own small business. But, maybe I just want to work in a non-profit making a difference somewhere in a distant country.
>
> I try not to be discouraged for not knowing what I want to do yet (outside of track and field). My journey is my own and I'll be enjoying it as it unfolds. I do not know the way yet, but with each day a lamp in front of me will be lit, leading me toward my calling. I have faith in the plan.

Peace meditation challenge is found on page 58

Anthem 22

I love the question, "Who are you?"

I find it incredibly intriguing because it's ever-changing. Besides the obvious, constant stuff, like the fact that every living organism is full of, light, life, and love, we are all always evolving and just trying to figure out the answer.

Who are you? Who am I? What do I stand for? What do I want?

Not knowing where to start, I begin to answer this question by my basic needs. A soul who wants to be accepted, liked, and loved. Which still doesn't say WHO I am and says more about what I desire, what I need. I guess it's my favorite question because it's so hard to answer, and even when you think you are answering it, you're not.

Maybe it doesn't need to be any deeper than simply being light, life, and love. Calling myself an athlete, a sister, daughter, or friend are just titles. Maybe who you are isn't one answer. Maybe it is a compilation of all of our desires and needs, our goals and titles. They all as one make up who we are.

If that's the case, then I <u>am</u> a sister, daughter, and friend. I am a soul put on this Earth to love. I am a free spirit, a wanderer who makes a home wherever she lies her head. I wear my heart on my sleeve even though that has caused much heartache. I have loved a hundred times and I will continue to do so, because I am hopelessly romantic.

I am a fighter, always have been. I am brave. I pursue the things that make my heart race with fear. I am a walking contradiction. A vegetarian who occasionally eats meat. A bird that needs both a home and the open skies. I'll slap someone and kiss them at the same time. I'm unpredictable, but I'll always choose cupcakes over pie, red wine over white, left over right, unless of course we need to go left, then I'll probably choose right because my sense of direction is awful.

In all seriousness, I know I am not my name or my body. I am not what I do or what I've achieved. I am but a soul. Dust, come together so perfectly to create energy that we call life, with the sole purpose of growing, evolving, healing, and creating a better future.

That's who I think I am for now.... at least for today.

With love,
Mee

Anthem 23

YOU are the anthem. The life you live in praise, appreciation, and in honor of you and your magnificence IS the anthem. However, you choose to remind yourself of that is up to you.

In the late hours of the night, on a slow Sunday afternoon, or at the back of the runway preparing to jump, I found myself reciting the Tori Anthem.

My name is Tori Franklin. I am loved beyond measure. I am vibrant, loving energy created from the magical dust of stars. I am not unlovable because of my past. I am worthy, my body is worthy, and I love me, just the way I am, *including* everything I've been through. I attract light, joy, and abundance in all ways. To the me as I am today, I forgive you. To the me who was broken, abandoned, and ashamed, I love you.

Mee :)

Find the Forgiveness Challenge on page 61

"Laying here in the grass with my eyes closed I feel like I'm floating. The grass prickling my skin and my arms reaching above my head to the sunlight. It feels like the sun is stretching me. When I lift my legs to the sky, my feet feel the warmth. They dance as if tapping on the sun's rays."

– Tori Franklin

Challenge 1:
Be Present

Many people know meditation as sitting cross-legged, eyes closed, and silently humming "OM". In some circumstances it is, but meditation is really just a tool to bring your mind back to the present moment. Anything can be a form of meditation, writing, dancing, even eating. Take this challenge one day at a time. Focus on just one really intentional day to BE PRESENT. From the moment you wake up, be present. Meditate or pray on being aware of everything you are doing, of feeling every sensation, and being there mentally, physically, and spiritually for it. Actively think *I am here*. All throughout the day.

Any part of your day can be a meditation. As you brush your teeth don't think about what you will have for breakfast, focus on brushing your teeth. Focus on how the bristles feel against your gums. As you shower, rejoice in the warmth of the water on your skin and be THERE. Driving to work, doing your work, eating lunch, ACTUALLY taste it, feel it in your mouth. Don't go through the motions. Whatever it is you are doing be present mentally as well. Your mind should be focused on the task, and if your mind drifts off and you need a little reminder say to yourself, *I am here*.

Doing this can make your day more productive because your attention is on the one thing you're doing without distraction from your own mind. And if you are relaxing for the day, completely relax. If you choose to use your mind to reflect and think about things, then do it with intention. Turn off the television, put down your phone, and reflect. When it comes time to swipe on an app, do that with intention too.

All day I want you to say to yourself *I am here.* Life is too short to be anywhere other than where you are at this moment. At the end of the day, think about how you did. Do you feel like you remembered to be present, or were there gaps in the day when you were on autopilot and weren't paying any attention? Whether you feel you did it well or not, try it again the next day. Reflect at the end of the day, then do it all over again.

I'm leaving space below for you to mention things that you noticed within your *presence* that maybe you aren't usually aware of when you're on autopilot.

For example: I never noticed that I don't actually enjoy the flavor of the cereal I eat every morning.

Or

When I'm more present, traffic doesn't seem so daunting. I'm able to calm myself.

Challenge 2:
Develop a Loving Gaze

When was the last time you got completely naked and looked at yourself? I don't mean looked at yourself and thought about all the things you dislike. But, really looked and admired yourself from the perspective of someone who loves you. That's the next activity.

Find a time when you can be alone and undress. Before you go running to the mirror, sit somewhere in a comfortable position. Close your eyes and rest your hands gently on your knees or in your lap, palms facing the sky. Keep your spine tall yet relaxed, and slowly rotate your neck in circles as you take a few deep breaths to silence your mind. Try to align your breathing to your movement. Breathing in when your head leans back, nose to the ceiling, and out when your head circles the front of your body. Do both directions.

Bring your head back to center and begin rotating your spine, breathing in a similar fashion. Breathe in as you push your chest forward and out as your back hunches over. Then switch directions. Wiggle your toes and touch your fingertips to your palm and tap your thumb to each of your fingertips. Be present for these sensations. Continue your breathing and come to stillness. Fill your lungs to capacity then completely empty them, in through your nose and out through your mouth. Repeat this three times, then return to a regular breathing pattern.

Feel your body's presence and thank it for all it does for you. Imagine a love bubble around you, pink and shiny. Breathe in this love and allow it to flow through your body. Feel its energy coursing through your veins to every corner of you. Tell your body that you love it.

I know that for some, this may feel unnatural, uncomfortable, or just untrue. We have these preconceived thoughts about our body already ingrained in our minds. Speaking these statements of love and appreciation for our body is not something we do often, let alone actually believe when we do. When these feelings of discomfort arise, or when the thoughts negating all the positive self-talk show themselves, acknowledge it and say, "Just because I feel this way or am having these thoughts does not make them true." These are conditioned thoughts and they have no validity. Let these thoughts go and replace them with kindness. Replace this discomfort with feelings of love. Continue to work on it. Your self-image may not change in one day; it will be something you need to practice again and again.

Once finished, with a new loving gaze, go to your mirror and look upon yourself. Witness all of your beauty and power and light as someone who adores you. Take a good look at your long toes, your cankles, up to your knobby knees, or your thunder thighs. Look at your belly and the folds at your waist, look at your bird chest or your uneven breasts, your skinny shoulders and to the back. See your wide hips and your stretch-marked ass. Look at the cellulite on your hamstrings and down to your big feet again. See it all and embrace it all; with this eye of a lover, love it all.

Challenge 3:
Reflecting on a Low Point

We all have those days when it feels like the weight of the galaxy is on our shoulders. When it takes all that we have just to get out of bed, and some days we don't even make it that far. Think about the last time that happened to you. What were your worries in the days leading up to it? Were you stressed about work or a project coming up? Was there a family gathering in the near future? Someone you weren't keen on seeing going to be in proximity to you? Was the worry of paying bills on your mind? Fear of the future and your goals, or lack thereof? Write down what was most on your mind leading up to your last low point. These are called triggers.

_____

_____

_____

_____

_____

_____

Next, was there one particular trigger that sent you overboard? Was there that one moment when you couldn't hold yourself together anymore? The moment when everything crumbled within you. Was it a song that reminded you of a lover long ago? Did someone call out an insecurity of yours? Did you receive another bill in the mail? Were you watching everyone on social media acquire all that you desire? Write down what it was that caused the scale to tip.

_____

_____

_____

_____

_____

_____

_____

_____

Then think about what thoughts you were having during that period. What were the words replaying over and over in your head? The nasty, mean, untrue lies you tell yourself, sometimes automatic. *"I'm worthless!" "I hate you!" "I'm such a loser!" "Everyone hates me! Nobody likes me!" "I'm ugly and pathetic!"* Write them down here before continuing with the reading!

_____

_____

_____

_____

_____

_____

_____

_____

I want you to know that these thoughts that come into your mind do not define you. These emotions that come and go do not make you who you are. Even with all your flaws and things to improve upon, you are perfect as you are. Perfectly imperfect. How does it feel reading that- do you crave to hear those words or do they feel untrue?

The things you love less about yourself are things that make you unique. They are the things that make you spicy! Interesting! And as to the things that you are able to improve on, do so with a loving mindset and compassion along the way.

Challenge 4:
Moving Through Emotions Meditation

This meditation is specifically for when you feel yourself slipping. When the negative thoughts are coming more consistently, and the breakdown is imminent. This is to help you climb out of that black hole and clear away the dark, suffocating, cloud of misery.

Calm your breathing. In through your nose, deep and slow. Feel your ribcage expand and imagine all of the oxygen molecules circulating through your body. Breathe out through your mouth. Keep going, even if it seems difficult at first. Think about whatever emotion it is you are feeling. Whether it be anger, sadness, self-pity, loneliness, and say to yourself, *"I feel anger. I am not angry." "I feel worthless. But, I am not worthless."* By separating yourself from the emotion it gives you space to see it as it is, an emotion, a fleeting sensation. You do not need to identify as this feeling, you are not Anger. You are not Sadness. You are not Loneliness. You are not Worthless. You are merely experiencing this emotion, in this moment.

As your breathing begins to slow, take a few moments to feel your body. Feel where the pain resides. Is it near your throat? Do you feel a stiffness in your heart? Does your gut ache? Where is the tension within your body? Once you've located it, gently place your hands over this space and breathe deeply into it. In your mind's eye, imagine each breath expanding this area. With every breath it grows until the space completely opens. In through your nose, out through your mouth. As you breath out allow your breath to turn into sound. It may come out as a moan, a scream, or a song like sigh. Continue with this sound. Allow the sound to open the space within you.

If you can't find the specific area, rest your hands beside you, palms facing up and do the breathing above into your entire body. Allowing your breath to open everything within you along its way.

While you continue your deep breathing, feeling the oxygen flow through your body, tell yourself, "*I am safe. I am in a safe place.*" Speak to the inner child that is feeling all of this so deeply. Tell your little you, "*We are safe. I will take care of you.*" And trust that you have the ability to do that. Trust that you can take care of your emotional needs.

Tell yourself, "*I love you.*" You can say it in your head, you can whisper it, or you can say it out loud. As you do, tell it to the inner you that aches. The you that is in pain in this moment. Tell yourself, "*I love you,*" over and over until you know it's true.

Challenge 5:
Peace Meditation

Meditation has many purposes, and I want you to try this *at least* three times this week, two separate mornings and once in the evening. I say two in the morning because it's good to start the day with a clear mind and positive energy. It will make any mishap or misstep that comes throughout the day less significant. You'll be able to respond from a place of peace - not react from a space of tension.

Set your morning alarm fifteen minutes earlier than usual. Right as you awaken, after you've turned off your alarm but before you check your emails, social media, or text messages, sit up into a comfortable position. I like to sit cross-legged with my teddy bear, Leo, propped up and facing me, like we are meditating together. I pull my comforter up over my shoulders because it's typically chilly in the morning, and I'm not quite ready to let go of its warmth. This position alone makes me smile just a bit. Find your comfortable, happy position.

This could be sitting on the edge of your bed, knees shoulder width apart, toes gently touching the ground. You could sit on the floor, legs spread out like a starfish and back resting against the wall, or you could go to a chair in your room and get comfortable there. Whatever this position is for you, make sure you aren't slouching, your shoulders are relaxed, your head is up with your jaw unclenched.

Take the first few minutes just to breathe (you don't need to time it, just feel what seems right). Deep, slow, even breaths. Try not to think about what you have to do for the day. Don't think about the errands you need to run, or the kids, the activities, nor the assignments due. Simply breathe, allow your entire body, your entire mind to relax. Feel yourself sitting in your room at this exact moment. If your mind wanders, pinpoint that thought in your mind, breathe into it and imagine it evaporating.

When you have found your place of peace, smile! This part of the exercise I adopted from one of my favorite books/movies, *Eat Pray Love*. Smile and let it not just be with your lips. Lighten your brows like you do when you're laughing. Drop your shoulders and imagine your entire body smiling with you, from your toes to your nose. And as Katut, the Balinese medicine man, said, "even smile in your liver." Take multiple deep, simple, happy, breaths here. Then begin to imagine the energy around you. What color is it? How does it feel? If you had to pluck words out of this misty aura, what would they be? As you breathe in, breathe in these words. Breathe in '*love*' then breathe out in silence. Breathe in '*joy*', breathe out with no thought in mind. Breathe in '*patience*'. Out. In '*empathy*'. Out. In '*confidence*' and so on. Choose words you would like to facilitate into your life for the day. And if a word doesn't come to mind right away, don't stress it. Take a few in silence and until one flows to you naturally.

You will start to feel your energy shifting into a lighter, easier, happier space. By breathing in these positive thoughts, you are manifesting a world in which these things thrive for yourself. When you are finished, take a couple more minutes in silent breath. Be at peace.

For the evening meditation, you can do the same activity. The purpose is to rid your mind of the stresses of the day and go into your rest happy and peaceful.

"We are shaped by our thoughts; we become what we think. When the mind is pure, joy follows like a shadow that never leaves."

– Buddha

Challenge 6:
Forgiveness

Forgiveness can be a difficult task to achieve. We think that the people who hurt us don't deserve to be forgiven or haven't asked us for forgiveness so why should we. We have trouble forgiving ourselves because we can't let go of what we did (or didn't do). We hold onto it, all of it.

Yet the only one who suffers from withholding forgiveness is the one who can't let go. There are four key emotions that often block someone's ability to forgive. Shame. Blame. Guilt. Anger. Sometimes it can be difficult to decern which of these we are feeling. Before we can even begin to forgive another person, we must first be open to forgiving ourselves.

In the chart below write what you are feeling about each of these emotions. In the shame box, write what you are ashamed about. In the blame box write what you believe you are to blame for and so on. You may not have a response for every box, but whichever ones you are feeling, this will be a good way to see what you're holding on to.

Shame	Blame
Guilt	Anger

I challenge you to begin the process of forgiveness. Forgive yourself. Forgive yourself for saying yes. Forgive yourself for saying no or for not being able to speak at all. Forgive yourself for being there in the first place. Forgive yourself for not being able to stop it or for starting it. Forgive yourself for keeping it to yourself or for telling everyone. Forgive yourself for the feelings you wish you didn't have. Whatever it might be, you must forgive yourself.

It's the little things you tell yourself that slowly begin to change your mind. You have your chart here. Picture one of the moments clear in your mind and connect with the 'you' that experienced it. Not the you who is here reading this… the one who is still in that memory, reliving that moment over and over. Speak to that part of you. Take three deep, slow breaths and on the exhale whisper "*I forgive you*".

Do this with each box that you have written something in. Take your time. This activity may need to be done multiple times for the forgiveness to set it. Once it has, you can then begin to extend your forgiveness to others. Who do you blame? Who has angered you?

Go to those moments in your mind and send this person love and compassion. It may be very difficult to do this, but by sending this person love and compassion, you are sending the same to yourself. You are allowing yourself freedom from the choke hold this anger, guilt, blame, or shame has on you. Give it time and keep trying.

It's natural for this activity to be unsettling and raise strong emotional reactions. That's all part of the process of letting go. Be sure to have emotional support available. Whether that be a family member, close friend, or mental health professional.

Forgive yourself, so you can forgive them, so that you can be FREE

- How did the activity of letting go make you feel afterward?

- Did this challenge bring you any peace? Were you able to connect with the hurt part of you that needs forgiveness? If not, how can you go deeper to really speak to the part of you that needs to hear it?

Anyways,
 I Forgive You,
 Mee

Part Two

The Rise

Paris, France

Anthem 24

In order to live a fulfilling life, it starts with love and acceptance of self. All of you, including your pain. The pain you've endured has made you into who you are today. Let your pain become your power. This healing process begins in solitude but we ultimately have to apply these same concepts into our relationships with other people.

Before the Tokyo Olympics, I decided to move to Paris, France to continue my pursuit of greatness. I had big goals for my debut Olympic experience and I planned to give it everything I had. I wanted a coach who was organized, a coach that would push me to my limits, a coach that saw my goals as a realistic possibility for me. Maybe I was just looking for an adventure and a coach as crazy as I was. I left behind everything I own and everyone I love and moved across the world.

For the first month I lived in France, I spent most of my time alone. I would train, go home, sometimes go out for a chat at a cafe and have a glass of wine like a true Parisian. But I struggled to make any real friends.

My training group and I were on our way to a training camp in Tenerife, Spain. I watched them huddled together at the gate, talking in French and showing each other funny videos on social media. I thought about joining them, but a voice in my head reminded me that I wouldn't be able to understand what they were saying anyways. I grabbed my headphones from around my neck and put them over my ears, drowning out my exclusion.

I listened to the song Tenerife Sea by Ed Sheeran, excited to see the shades of blue he sang about. As I boarded the flight, I felt something 'off' in my spirit. A feeling of discontentment. Something so small but felt in the deepness of my silence, like a vertebra in the spine turned ever so slightly out of alignment. It bothered me for days.

I noticed myself aching for attention from my teammates. For no reason or purpose in particular, but my ego desired it… for them to look at me, smile at me, explain the joke to me, to care if I was around or not. Recognizing this, I tried to take a deep breath and release that energy. Some of it cleared, but I knew the ego was not easily defeated.

What I came to understand about myself, relative to this new group, was that I felt lonelier around them than I did alone. Being around them made me think about my friends and my family, reminiscing about the laughs and how I used to feel when I was with them. Watching the group interacting with one another made me miss laughing, joking, having discussions, telling stories… all of which were very difficult for me to do with them. So, I further separated myself.

When we are in the midst of negative self-talk or a depressive state, we often keep our distance from others. We feel like we have to do things on our own, suffer on our own, because a small part of us thinks we deserve it.

I thought it would make me feel better to distance myself from the group, but it really only masked the underlying issue. I was a stranger, and I had made myself an outsider. Secluding myself didn't help them get to know me any better, nor did it encourage them to want to teach me French or try to understand when I butchered their language. My feelings of isolation had nothing to do with the team and everything to do with my ego's craving for attention and acceptance. The craving caused me to react in fear and flee into exile, only making the situation worse. I needed to face the feeling. I had to strengthen my connection with the team.

When I was with them and felt this sense of 'being an outsider', I recognized it in the moment. When they burst into laughter and I seemed to have missed the joke, I simply appreciated their joy. I welcomed their love for one another, embraced it as my own, and felt their positive energy even though it was not directed at me. I stopped allowing my ego to run rampant and I was able to love their company as it was. I accepted that in time I would get to know them, and they me.

Forcing myself into the mix made all the difference in the process of integration into the group, the French culture, to life overseas, and the country in general. Everyone feels like an outsider sometimes. Instead of running away in fear, lean into it and join in. It is through people that we can become more resilient, it is through connection that we can learn to express our true light and love.

In order to really grow on this quest of healing you have to be willing to put yourself in moments of discomfort, to try something you've never done before, to think in a way you've never thought. We create these stories in our mind based on our self-perception, but if I had merely been vulnerable with the group and expressed these feelings, they could have helped me out of those negative thoughts.

Take one day at a time and don't be too hard on yourself when you don't feel your best. With every lesson learned you've developed the tools needed to pull yourself out of the dirt. Each time you'll do it a little quicker, and a little easier.

Anthem 25

I didn't know what I was getting myself into when I packed my life into two suitcases and moved away from everything I'd ever known. I took for granted the luxuries of familiar grocery stores, street signs that were easy to comprehend, and most importantly, a language that's understood from coast to coast. Most of us are born and raised in the same environment. I tried to grow and develop in that space, but looking back on it now, I had to leave the confines of my country, my cradle, to further my growth. A country that sheltered me from "unapproved" cultures, traditions, languages, and food.

I thought I knew what the world was like because I lived in a "diverse" neighborhood, or watched the Amazing Race or one of those world-food tv shows. But I could never have known how sheltered I was until I left my home.

When I moved to France, I had to become a new version of myself. Everything I was no longer applied to the life I was living. I had to evolve. The very language I was born to know and understand no longer communicated what I needed it to. The foods I used to eat weren't available. The way I interacted with people wasn't received the same way. My old way of being no longer served its purpose. I had to change and adapt.

Even the way I spent my leisure time changed. I didn't have friends to call for a random trip to Sacre Coeur, a church that sits at the highest point of Paris with the most captivating views; I went alone, unsure of how to get there or what I would do when I arrived. With only myself to look in awe at the beauty of the scene, my thoughts became my companion. I laughed only to myself, argued with myself about where to eat or what direction to go, got excited on my own when passing a patisserie or frustrated with myself when I got lost along the way.

At times it was lonely to pass a storefront window and see only my reflection. It took some introspection and a change of mind to see my reflection and think, "that woman is actually a delight. I love spending time with her…and she's damn cute too." I began to see this time to myself as a period of growth instead of a period of isolation, a time of mental, emotional, and spiritual expansion instead of social confinement.

I moved to France to chase my dream of winning the Tokyo Olympics. I'm working under a coach that has one of the farthest jumps in the entire universe, and an ego to match. I say that in the most loving way. He pushes our minds and bodies in ways I've never been challenged before. From warm up drills, to lifting, to the very way I jump.

This, too, requires a 'me' that I have not been in the past. A 'me' that has yet to exist, but now is necessary to adapt. He tells me often that the goals I have are impossible for the person I am now. He requires me to make changes to the way I think about triple jump, training, competing, and what it actually takes to beat the world's best.

Changing the way you think is not an easy process. It takes constant work, noticing when you start to slip into old mental patterns, reminding yourself that this way of being or thinking will not serve you. If I'm being honest, the process is taxing. Not only am I trying to physically make my body do things that people don't normally do, but I'm also being pushed mentally to the brink of exhaustion.

I guess it leaves me asking myself, is it all worth it? Or would I rather be back at home, in my crib of a country, comfortable and settled, forever wondering if I had what it takes?

Anthem 26

When a person decides to become a coach, they take on the immense responsibility of shaping an athlete. They can help that person be their best self or potentially their worst.

We always discuss the mental health of the athletes and help them to overcome fear and self-doubt, but the conversation rarely ventures into the mental Olympics that coaches go through. The imposter syndrome, the fear of failure, their mistaken identification with their own personal accomplishments or successes as an athlete and coach.

Coaches gossip and whisper as much as high school kids do. Saying who doesn't know what they're talking about, who's had a one-hit wonder, which coach is too arrogant, which coaches are over or underrated.

Then there is pressure from their universities or national governing bodies. Are they getting the recognition they feel they deserve, the support they desire? Are sponsors taking notice of them?

If their own insecurities are not quelled, they will pass this fear and pressure down onto their athlete. They will subconsciously (and sometimes consciously) sabotage both themselves and the athletes. They will tell the athlete they are not ready, when really it is the coach themself who does not believe they can get them ready.

Athletes shouldn't leave a coach feeling depressed, incompetent, or lost. Narcissism in a coach is the most toxic poison for an athlete.

All this is to say… it's not enough to know your sport or event. It isn't enough to be technically knowledgeable or know the ins and outs of training cycles. A coach must be self-aware enough to recognize their own insecurities and fears and find a way to self-heal and self-soothe. They have to be open to listening, learning, and recognize the influence they have on their athlete's mental health.

More importantly, the coach should know that they are not defined by their failures or successes. They are not defined by what judgments other people pass about their coaching abilities or personal decisions. They are more than just a coach. They are complex people and should give themselves grace and the space to heal.

Anthem 27

March of 2021 – Olympic Year

My coach: "Do you think she's going to medal?"

My coach's assistant: "Well, no, but she's a strong jumper…"

"I'm not excited to coach you anymore. I don't want to coach you. If someone were to ask me today if I would coach Tori Franklin, I would say no."

"You don't have the mindset to medal at championships."

"You are not a fighter."

"You're a good woman. You are the fucking light, you're a good good woman. It's not personal, but professionally we do not match."

"For the goal you said you wanted to achieve, I don't think it will happen. We are late. Mentally, we are too late."

"It's not that I don't think you won't jump 15 meters. I know you can. You fast. Strong. You have all the things. You have all the things. It doesn't matter who coach you. You could coach yourself to 15.20, but the way I think and work and the way you think and work is not good."

"We have a good relationship now but down the line I don't know. So, I rather end it now."

"Your weakness is you don't take anything seriously enough. To you everything gone be ok.

"I'm never wrong about triple jump. If I have to make a list of who is on the podium. You wouldn't be on it."

This is what my coach said to me today. He no longer wants to coach me. I had a feeling he was upset with me, so to begin our hour-long conversation I asked him not to give up on me. He responded with the statements above. I went to the bathroom to release the tears I was holding back, then we went to practice. I was hurt by some of the things he said, but I wasn't sad so much. I was mostly just pissed off. I'm still pissed off. Fuck him. I don't want to be under a coach that feels that way about working with me.

I ain't no weak bitch. He mistakes my vulnerability, kindness, and positivity for weakness. I ain't never been. He fucked up. Cuz I'm the shit.

He said my mind is not ready to win an Olympic Gold Medal.
He says I'm not a fighter.
He just created a monster.

How can I use this to improve my mindset? How can I have the mind of a champion? And is it true that mine is not one? Am I capable of coaching myself? Could I do that?

Anthem 28

I've started talking with coaches to see who would be willing to coach me on such short notice. I'm talking to coaches in Greece, New York, Michigan, and possibly Florida.

Last night, I spoke with my sports psychologist. I told her all the things he said and the full background story as to why. She helped me take what is true from the conversation and recognize what we could throw out, which was most of it. She just reminded me that I'm a boss-ass Queen and I don't need that shit. Not her words exactly, I'm paraphrasing.

Shit is real right now though. The Olympic games are right around the corner. Any decision I make right now will affect the outcome. It woke me up. This whole situation woke me up.

This has been my dream, my goal, for 12 years. When I was younger, it was merely to make the Olympic team, but that isn't the case anymore. I have what it takes to get Gold, to get fucking GOLD, but I haven't been putting everything else on hold to achieve that. I can't do ANYTHING else. The time is NOW. I am right here in this moment and everything I do affects what will happen there. I need to be ready. I have all the tools. My mind is strong. I am a fighter. I have the champion mentality.

Anthem 29

I've wanted to write, but I find it very difficult to do. It's exhausting to keep explaining the story to everyone. Trying to tell it so that it makes sense when it inherently doesn't. I've told the people close to me in waves. Every few days or so, when I have the energy. I just haven't really felt like talking about it though. It makes me sad. I don't want to leave Paris…but I'm trying hard to let it go. That's what life is about, huh, acceptance and letting go. I do accept that this is happening, I just can't believe it. It's crazy.

My emotions vary. I cried a little the first few days, but not since, not about the situation at least. The last two days have been hard, but I'm holding myself together. I'll break eventually and let it all out, just a matter of time. I'm just so preoccupied with packing, cancelling my internet and other bills, selling my $200 refrigerator for $75, my $350 washing machine for $100, and giving away my $800 mattress for free. I'm struggling to find a place to live, while trying to say goodbye to the few friends I made here. I haven't had much time to grieve.

Some days I find myself stress sleeping. When I feel overwhelmed by the smallest task I just start crying, groan, and collapse onto my bed. I curl into a ball and sleep. I don't eat much during these times.

My best friend gave me good advice. "Don't worry about all the things you have to do, just focus on this next hour. What do you need in order to function and feel steady so that you can get one thing done." I needed to feed myself. So, for twenty minutes of that hour, I ate, and after that I was able to return to my to-do list. It helped.

Today was my last day in Paris, and I actually had a really nice day alone. This morning I ran some errands at Monoprix, a chain grocery store similar to Target. I needed to buy more suitcases because I've accumulated way more clothes here than I came with. I shipped my books to my sister and then ate lunch and tried to take a nap.

Sometimes I feel like I don't have a home. But I know home is where the heart is, as lame as that saying is. I guess since mama is in Chicago, it'll always be home. I just feel like I'm always moving, like I can't ever get settled anywhere. I was hoping to stay here for a few years… but alas, life strikes again.

After many long conversations, I'm going to train with Donald Scott and his coach Sterling Roberts in Ypsilanti, Michigan. I've known Donald for eight years now, and I've gotten to know his coach a bit as well. I know I'm going somewhere I'll be supported and surrounded by people who not only care about me as an athlete, but as a person. That's really what I need right now.

I want to remember everything I learned here. Everything I learned from my previous coaches, everything I've learned from my physio, and create a jumping style that is unique to me. That gives me leverage over everyone. That changes the fucking game.

At my level of competitiveness, I shouldn't be making the technical mistakes that I do. I need to be better. I need to level up. I need to be obsessed, a professional, a fucking monster. I fully believe

I'm the only jumper who can rival those who have dominated the field. But I can't do it the way I am now. I can't fucking do it the way I am now!

I want to cry and punch shit and scream. I want to dance and have sex and love. I want to rip out my throat and never speak again. My heart wants to burst....my heart just wants to burst.

I <u>know</u> I can do this, I'm just a little tired of all these obstacles. But ima keep going.
I have to.

Anyway, I love you,
Boss Ass Bitch

Anthem 30

My last few hours in Paris went really smoothly. I woke up at 8am and finished packing and cleaning, and then my friend Neona came over to take my bike, YaYa, and my two plants, Joan and Mercy. I believe they will be well taken care of. She's a digital artist, and she gave me a print of one of her pieces.

After she left, the landlord came to check the place out. He was really nice today; I was surprised because the last time we talked he was a real asshole when my apartment had a rat infestation last month. He made me pay for my own exterminators. How Parisian, right? But he helped me take out my trash and move all my bags out of my apartment. He also agreed to ship my rug to the U.S for me. I was going to just throw it out, but I really do love that rug.

Now I'm on my flight back to Chicago. Side note, my luggage cost 2,245 euros! That made me even more angry at my ex-coach for being such a prick.

I'm feeling a lot right now, but mostly sad. I'm going to miss the team and the friends I've made. And I just feel like my journey in Paris wasn't finished, like there was more for me to do there. And I don't mean all the museums I didn't get to visit or all the vegan places I didn't get to try… I just mean for my growth.

But I know I can grow anywhere if I'm open to it. Just gotta keep taking life as it comes. Life has a way of uprooting us, of taking our plans and shitting on them. Sometimes we don't like the detour, but I like to believe that ultimately, we are shown something better.

I have to believe that I received what I came here for. I learned what I needed to from Paris, from my ex-coach, from my experiences. The universe has decided that this stage is over and it's time for the next level.

Ann Arbor, Michigan

Anthem 31

Post Tokyo Olympics

The 2021 Olympics was a test of my inner work. I finished my sixth and final attempt at the beautiful stadium in Tokyo Japan. I wiped the dust off my legs and looked back at the mark in the sand behind me. I could tell immediately that it wasn't far enough to qualify for the triple jump finals and fight for a medal. My Olympic journey was finished.

I left the stadium and found my coach at the warm-up track. He wanted to talk about what just happened but I told him, "I don't want to say anything right now, because if I do, it will not be from my highest self." He understood and walked me to the bus that would take me to the Olympic village. I did my best to stop any and all thoughts that arose in that moment because I KNEW they would not be positive. Knowing this, I did it anyways. I pulled out my phone and wrote them ALL DOWN. Every toxic and false thought racing through my mind, I wrote them all down.

In my practice of mindfulness and awareness of my thoughts I knew these were fleeting and false, but they needed an outlet in that moment, so I let them speak.

"Everyone was pulling for me and I fucking blew it. I'm embarrassed. I'll just disappear now…just disappear. I can't believe I just did that. I'm mad at myself. I don't even want to train anymore. I obviously don't perform well at championship meets. Don't know why, just seems to be a pattern. I don't feel like an Olympian anymore. I don't want the OLY after my name. I don't feel like I deserved it and I don't want it as a consolation prize. All of this was stupid! What am I even doing this for?? Why would God guide me to France just to be kicked out of my training group, send me to MiChiGaN, where I retrained my mindset, MADE the Olympic team, flew to fucking TOKYO, only to get 13th place and go the fuck back to... Michigan.

I might as well let the ants eat me; it would be my greatest purpose in this life to be the nourishment of the ants. That's how I feel. Empty, purposeless, nothing left of me but a shell, worthy only of maggots."

Looking back on it now, it all seems humorous and overdramatic, but those were all genuine emotions that needed to be let out. I needed that unfiltered moment to vent without trying to force myself away from them. I laid in bed for thirteen hours the next day, feeling it all. Crying, eating old cake I'd saved, watching terrible rom-coms, and crying some more.

I would've stayed there the entire day if it hadn't been for my family reaching out to me. I didn't respond to any of them, but those closest to me sent me videos and lengthy paragraphs reminding me how much they love me, how great it is that I had the courage enough to pursue this dream, and that my performance does not dictate my worth. With each message, the words slowly began to sink in and I was able to pull myself together and face the world. I remembered that my life and career are more than this moment. Yes, the Olympics can be considered the pinnacle of track and field, but it's not all there is. There are indoor and outdoor World Championship meets almost every year. They too consist of the world's BEST athletes and I need to be ready for them. I could sit and cry over this, or I can set new goals.

The old me would've believed all the negative things I'd written and would not have gotten out of the bed. The old me would have her confidence shattered for months, if not years, and would have tried to handle it all on her own. Progress is progress and its baby steps like this that make me proud of myself.

I obviously still have low days. Self-healing is not a one-stop shop. It's full of twists and turns and sometimes it will feel like you're back at rock bottom. The important thing is not to stay there.

Anthem 32

The difference between me in 2018 when I jumped the American record and me now is that I had unrelenting self-confidence. I just knew I was going to compete well and have fun doing it. Recently I've been too wound up, too worried about doing everything right, too hung up on results and expectations. Little by little, it all ate at my belief in my ability to achieve the things I set out to do.

I think it's obviously good to have goals, but for now, I think I need to set them aside. Right now, my only focus needs to be taking everything one day at a time, moment by moment, and spending these moments as my absolute best self. Giving *this* moment everything I have. And in the end that will be enough. It will always be enough, no matter the result.

Anthem 33

I am feeling much better since the games, but I must admit sadness still comes in waves. I'm allowing them to come and go.

I'm currently on a flight to Maui, Hawaii for an offseason vacation. I talked to two people during my travels today. My Uber driver, a bald, overweight 65-year-old man, got caught in the winds of telling me all about his dating life. He'd been married twice. The first time was when he was very young. They were together for twenty years, had kids, eventually grew apart, and divorced. He said they stopped talking to each other and just didn't know each other anymore.

The second marriage was with a woman fifteen years younger than him. He kept telling her it would never work, but she was persistent. At the end of the day, he was glad that she was, because even though their age difference was great, they still had much in common and learned a lot from one another. She was different in a way that he'd never met in anyone else. When she turned thirty, she passed away from cancer. He was there with her every step of the way.

He then told me that dating ever since has been kind of a joke. The women have lied and just not been in alignment with him. Now he's dating a lady he loves, but she's crazy and every other month they break up. He says at that age you just enjoy what you have.

I also spoke with an 82-year-old woman. She was thin, almost opaque, and had frail hands with bruises on them. She had the sweetest demeanor and really wanted to chat. She told me about her husband passing and how sudden his heart attack was. She later asked me what I do, and got so excited when she found out I was an "Olympic person", and we talked a lot about the Olympics, difficulties of being an athlete, mental health, and her children.

I asked her what she feels is the one lesson she's learned through her years on this Earth. She said, "Just take it one day at a time. Sometimes you do your best and it just isn't enough, but that's okay because you did your best. Either way, the sun will still rise tomorrow."

Enjoy what you have while you have it, and it take it one day at a time. The sun will rise tomorrow.

Words from the wise.

Love,
Mee

Anthem 34

I feel like I've been moving around, traveling, on my feet, seeing people, dancing, drinking, training, talking, laughing, crying.... nonstop crying. Doing it all non-stop for the entire year.

The last time I really slowed down was in my off-season last year when I fasted. I haven't had any real alone time or peace since Tokyo. I'm tired. I'm sad. I just want some time without someone asking me how Tokyo was or telling me how exciting the experience must have been. Don't ask me how I am because I don't know. I just want to be left alone, to get away and be something else for a little while.

I recently finished a book called Spiritual Yoga. It was about a religious practice called Krishna Consciousness. They worship Krishna, a Hindu god, as their version of God, the Universe, the All-Mighty Jah.

I've only read one book about it so far, so I am by no means an expert, but it focuses a lot on detachment and pursuing ultimate sense gratification. By detachment I mean from pretty much anything that is related to this world. Releasing our desires for money, cars, clothes, status, even your family and personal identity. Ultimate sense gratification is letting go of anything that you do/have in your own self-interest. Which I think at some level has always been my aim.

92

Many charities, philanthropists, and religious people only work for certain communities, societies, and countries. This is called extended sense-gratification. Krishna Consciousness talks about how this isn't great, because it makes you choose one community over another. When pursuing ultimate sense gratification, you serve a higher power (Krishna, God, etc.), and in turn you serve all communities. By doing this we ultimately serve ourselves. This is the only way to appease all.

There are other standard things in the practice, like no sex, no eating meat, no drinking, no gambling.... I already follow 2 of those 4 things. Hah.

I'm not saying I'm converting or anything, but I find it interesting to read about. It makes me think about things differently, so I'll see where the journey takes me.

Anthem 35

I had my first appointment with my therapist since before I left for the Olympics. It was a really good session, as most of them have been. I started by telling him about my Olympic experience, which was interesting because while I've talked to friends and listened to everyone's supportive comments, I've dealt with it mostly on my own. Over the past few weeks, I've found my way to a mostly healthy and stable mental space.

Our conversation didn't shake me up too much, but I did feel a little bit of that sadness and disappointment. He mentioned how proud of me he was for how I've handled this experience, and how I handled the year in general. Then he left me with some advice…

"The best thing you can do for yourself is to accept it. The way you'll learn and grow from it, is to accept that it happened and how it happened. You need to understand the lesson from it all, and figure out a way to be better from having had that experience."

Anthem 36

Today my therapist shared an interesting observation. He said a child looks for stability externally, because when they are young, they rely on their parents and adults to protect them, give them security, and provide a safe home. They need these external factors to feel safe and stable.

My lifestyle requires that I move around a lot. I go from place to place, and as an adult I don't NEED one home or external factor to feel 'safe'. I can find my stability internally, ground myself, or find a safe place in a person I trust.

But the kid in me still sometimes looks for stability externally. Sometimes I feel moments of anxiety because my inner child is saying she's scared, she doesn't feel secure. I have made sure that I am safe and taken care of, and it is my job as an adult to remind the child in me that we are ok.

When I had to leave Paris, adult me made arrangements, found a coach, found a home, and made sure we (my inner child and me) were safe. But the child in me was still afraid. That's why I refused to unpack once I was settled... little me was afraid of getting too comfortable and possibly having to uproot again.

He said, if the child is in charge it will fight, push back, or try to run when it is afraid. It will look for shelter, because that's what kids do. But when the adult you is in control, the child may be afraid but she will push forward as she has so many times before. It's all just a matter of recognizing who is speaking and who is afraid, who needs to be reassured so we can keep moving forward.

All the things that I'm afraid of, I can do and handle, whatever the outcome.

He also used a really cool metaphor:
"Often when people are terrified of something, they liken it to standing on a ledge. They cry and scream and refuse to look down because they don't want to jump. They give up.

Eventually they hype themselves up and take the leap, only to find that the depth was only six inches. It was merely a step. They breathe easy for a second, until it comes time to make the jump again. They get all pumped up to jump off the ledge once more, taking the leap, only to find it's just another step. Each time, it's merely a step closer to their goal. They're afraid, hooting and hollering about it, but when they actually make the leap, they realize it's not as far a drop as they think."

Anthem 37

I moved into my new apartment yesterday in Ann Arbor, Michigan. I spent all day today cleaning, unpacking and running back and forth to the store to get this place in order. There's still so much to do.

I've thought about whether or not to buy furniture a million times. I still have PTSD from all the money I spent on furniture in France, how much I bought in Chicago before that, and how I always end up leaving it behind. My best friend tried to reassure me that if I leave from here, it'll be by choice. I can leave if and when I want, and I can stay if I want. I still don't think I'll buy real furniture; the place is too small for that. But I did buy two yoga pillows for the floor.

I'm excited about the space I'm creating. I want my home to be a place of peace, grounding, warmth, and joyful playfulness. It's coming along.

Anthem 38

I'm locking my hair this Thursday, so this is my last week with an afro for who knows how long. I'll be starting a YouTube page to document the entire journey.

I'm excited, but I have noticed a bit of emotion come up when I talk about the effect my hair has had on me in competition and when I think about the little girls it has inspired.

My hair has always meant more to me than just some dead follicles on the top of my head. Through the years I nurtured, cherished, and silently watched as my hair grew and flourished. I have memorized every crimp and tried every style with my free natural afro. To me, the experience is about more than just styling and length retention. From a young age I likened my hair to my spiritual journey.

My first big chop was in high school. I had a perm which split my ends and thinned my hair. I'd just moved to a new school district with a population that looked significantly different than the former. I went from a predominantly white school to one that was much more diverse. In finally seeing more people who looked like me, I saw that I could be MORE of myself. I didn't have to fit in with bone straight hair. I learned that if I wanted to evolve in this environment, I needed to be completely comfortable and confident in my skin, so in an attempt to start fresh, I chopped off my hair. It sprung around two inches from my scalp in luscious, kinky curls.

I grew out of high school and into college and my tresses grew along with me, stretching to the middle of my back. But during my freshman year of college, I went through a deep depression that left me feeling worthless. I considered dropping out of college and ultimately fell into a series of unhealthy coping mechanisms. I was also flat-ironing my hair almost every weekend, slowly damaging all the progress I'd made.

I eventually brought myself out of this low state, but I realized I had a lot of self-work to do. I wrote down all of my traumas and insecurities, found a therapist, and the summer before junior year, seeking another fresh start, I chopped off my hair again. Only this time I cut it even shorter!

So began another period of spiritual, mental, and emotional growth. My hair growth became a visible symbol of the growth happening inside me.

All along, I knew that one day I would get dreadlocks. I saw getting locs as a maturing stage of life, but I knew then that I was far too young and indecisive to take on such commitment. My hair was still growing, there were still so many styles I hadn't tried, so many places to wander in the world, so many frogs to kiss, so many careers to choose from. I knew that when the day came for me to loc my hair I would be grounded mentally, physically, and spiritually. I would know what I want my life to look like. I would be confident in who I am. I would be ready to commit to a relationship, and I would be excited to do so. I didn't know when this day would come, but I knew I wasn't ready for it then.

It's been seven years since the last time I cut my hair, and in that time my hair has become a part of my brand. People recognize me because I'm the triple jumper that competes with my big 'fro and a white bow. When I do photoshoots or interviews, I'm usually asked to have my afro out and wild.

Honestly, I'm thrilled that my hair gets the love and attention that it does. I love when young girls message me and tell me that I inspired them to run, or play, or just BE with their natural hair out and flowing. I've been able to be that person in so many lives, and it absolutely makes my heart melt.

Now my hair has grown all the way down to my lowest rib. And even more important to me, my spiritual growth has matched my 'fro. I discovered who I am, what I represent, and the message I want to share with others. I understand that I am connected to everyone and everything. I can hear the whispers in the wind, feel the immense love from the sun, and gain knowledge from those who have come before me.

I've done so much inner work and healing over these last several years. While I still see a therapist once a week, it seems I've done as much as I can do at this moment. I'm at the pinnacle of what I can achieve with the knowledge that I have right now. So, it's time to learn again.

It's time for another fresh start.

For the last few weeks, I've done plenty of research on how to start, maintain, and wash locs. I looked up how many to get and how the number can correlate with how thick or thin you want them to be. I did some reading on its past and fell in love with its spiritual history.

Many ancient cultures and religions believed that the spirit leaves the body through the head. Through knotting, twisting, and tying the hair, they believed they could preserve more energy in the body, which would lead to greater amounts of physical and spiritual strength.

Locs take about 10 months to two years to mature and actually "lock." It's during this period that the need for *patience* of the process, *acceptance* of the "budding" stages (that may not look so neat), and *love* of your own experience comes into play. This mirrors spiritual growth.

My hope is that this new journey will continue to propel me forward in my spiritual growth and on the triple-jump runway as well. If there's one thing I've learned, it's that it's all connected!

As much as I love the impact my 'fro has had on those who've seen me compete with it, I'm excited to start my next hair journey. I can feel that this stage of my life will come with an abundance of love and personal achievements. Hopefully I can continue to inspire by living my life as freely as possible.

With Love,
Mee

Anthem 39

Why, hello there!

I just got back from Baltimore, where I had a public speaking gig for Nation United. It's a non-profit for girls of color who play lacrosse. Since the sport is predominately played by white people, the group connects those of color so they can have a community within the sport. I had massive anxiety about writing the speech this time. I didn't start it until the day before, and it wasn't completed until just before I walked on stage to give it. But of course, it was amazing and the girls freaking loved it. Seriously.

After I finished, they asked questions for thirty minutes. Deep questions. To finish, I went around the room as they told me things that they love about themselves. It was truly an amazing experience and lit my entire spirit up. Every time I do one of these events it reminds me that the anxiety is always worth it.

My spirit is feeling particularly great lately. I don't know if it's all the future plans I'm manifesting, or the fact that I've finally got my locs or what. I just feel like I know what I'm supposed to be doing right now in this chapter of my life.

Twenty-nine is coming up quickly. The last of my twenties. I'll do my birthday reflections soon, but for now I want to bask in this moment of peace and grounding.

I am so blessed and I thank God for all of it, for all that I am.

The full moon is near. It is time to seal in the growth and confirm the goals that I wish to manifest.

LOVE. ABUNDANCE. STABILITY. PEACE. GROWTH.

Let's stack some money… money will come to me in this chapter of my life.

My locs will mature quickly and sprout from my head.

My body will be healthy and strong. I will connect it to my mind. My form and technique will be easy.

I will love unconditionally. Myself. My partner. My family. My friends. All spirits and energies that I encounter.

I will gain and retain knowledge of healing and herbal medicines. My body will be able to do things it's never done before.

With Love,
Mee

Anthem 40

Lately I've been feeling called to learn the ancient technique of Reiki. Reiki is a Japanese form of energy healing, facilitated by the gentle "laying of hands" to reduce stress and anxiety, promote relaxation, and encourage emotional and physical healing. It isn't religious at all or connected to any demonic realm. It connects us to the universal energy, to our own Higher Self.

My instructor, John, is a forty-something white man with a strong Midwest accent. He smiles a lot and laughs at his own jokes. So far, it's been a lot of information and a really unique experience that is definitely going to need time to sink in.

The first day was mostly him talking and telling me about the history of Reiki. There is a lot of speculation about the original origins of Reiki, some saying it was first used by the Buddha in India and then later used by Jesus. Others take it further and say it comes from the Atlantis civilizations.

But it was confirmed that Reiki was rediscovered by Dr. Mikao Usui at the end of the nineteenth century in Japan. After surviving a near-death experience with cholera, Dr. Usui devoted his life to healing. He traveled to the holy mountains of Kurama and mediated, prayed, and sang for twenty-one days. God showed him a vision that gave him the keys to the ancient healing used by both the Buddha and Jesus. Upon his death, it was passed on by word of mouth from teacher to student for generations.

John told me of his experiences when teaching it, how clients have responded and the different techniques and uses for Reiki. Some clients want it simply to relax, some want energetic healing or release, and others use Reiki to help heal physical ailments ranging from stiff muscles to cancer.

At the end we did a session to help open my connection to the Universal Energy, so that it may flow through my hands to heal. I sat in a meditative state, clearing my mind. My eyes were closed as he centered himself behind me. He gently touched my shoulders, and my body lifted ever so slightly. Behind my closed eyes I saw what looked like little planets or eyes dancing around me. The thought, "I am going to heal communities, heal generations," came to me. My arms and legs prickled with goosebumps. I could feel every single hair on my body. It was as if ice cold water was running down my spine.

John said that when he touched me, he felt that energy too, and he saw mothers of all nationalities and creeds surrounding me, and that they began dancing.

Afterward we did a distance reiki session, in which we treated someone that we were not in proximity with. John received a request from a man in Minnesota who asked for his help.

We created a space for where the man would be laying if he were present, and we proceeded to treat him as if he were with us, placing our hands over the space where his head would be, where his torso would be, and so on. I had a vision while treating… it was like I was seeing through the man's eyes. He was slouched over, looking down at his stomach. It was really weird, and I can't explain it, but it was amazing.

Today, on day 2, we discussed more of the symbols used in Reiki... what they mean and how they're used. We talked about how when you raise your energy levels certain people and animals will naturally gravitate towards you, but also about the importance of setting boundaries and protecting your energy.

We discussed transcendence and how important healers and Reiki is going to be within the general public. Some hospitals are already beginning to offer Reiki as a form of treatment. More holistic clinics are popping up every day and true Healing is being done.

At the moment I feel pretty light and floaty. Like something deep within me wants to release. I felt it during my first session with John, but I ignored it. It's the feeling that, "If I go down this route or talk about this topic I will 100% burst into tears, and I'd just rather not", ya know?

The following day we did my level two atonement, and it was beautiful. We again began by coming to a place of peace, a quiet meditative state with my eyes closed. Again, John placed his hands on my shoulders. This time I saw two shadows, and I saw a third shadow when he placed his hand on the top of my head. The shadows stood before me, and as John continued, they began to brighten.

John brought my hands to a prayer position and placed them at my chest. My hands began to tingle, and the shadows brightened until they were a brilliant white light. All I could do was watch as the three lights merged into one.

The tingling in my hands intensified so much that my right hand went completely numb. I breathed more deeply. My posture straightening with each inhale. My spine grew tall and powerful. My back felt twice as long, my lungs twice as full. I opened my eyes.

John said that the shadows represented the heart, mind, and gut. These are places from which we make our life's decisions. Understanding each piece of the triad helps you to gain greater self-awareness into your emotions and decision making, and seeing them combine and go into light is amazing. It symbolizes my internal unification, so that I am not driven solely by one… not being over-analytical, not hyper-emotional, and not going only by that "gut feeling". I can connect all three to make sound decisions and not be torn in one direction or the other.

Afterwards we played a game to test our psychic abilities. We each wrote three names down on a piece of paper and handed them to each other. We then had to write whatever came to us about these names. I was nervous of course, of writing something wrong, but I did it anyway.

He wrote Barbara, Noel, and Carla. I was called to Noel first. She seemed important, a significant person in his life, and the word brunette came to me. Also heavy, not in weight, but emotionally. When thinking about Carla, the words unique, artsy, a teacher, and a friend to many came to me. For Barbara, I wrote Family. Kind, smiley, warm, sharp, blond haired. Then, as I was finishing, my eyes started to water and I almost began to cry. I wrote, "a sad story."

We traded back. He read over the notes I wrote beside each name. A smile creased his face as he looked up at me.

"Noel was my ex-girlfriend. We had a very passionate and intense relationship. She is brunette and we had a really tough breakup. I actually moved across the country after we ended things."

I was shocked. It must be a lucky guess, right??

"Carla is my sister. She is very much the artist of the family, very quirky and unique."

"Barbara is my mom. She is very kind and warm, truly the sweetest woman. What made you write sad story?"

"I don't know, I was just looking at the name and an intense feeling started in my chest. And the more I sat with it, the stronger it got. I actually almost started to cry. I guess I got a little scared and didn't wait to see what would come up. I stopped it and just wrote 'sad story'."

He looked at the paper and then up at me. "Well, she does have a tough history. My mother was in the holocaust. When she was very young, she saw her mother killed right in front of her. To this day she hasn't been able to let go of her childhood trauma."

I was in disbelief. He told me that everyone can do this if only they open themselves up and connect deeper within.

Anthem 41

I completed my final class today. I am officially a certified Reiki master. John was right, in that the last attunement would be the most interesting experience.

We started the day with him telling stories, per usual. We discussed the remaining symbols and their meanings. They're beautiful, definitely something I may want to tattoo someday.

I asked him questions about how he started his business and how he runs it, and about what he thinks about while giving treatment. But the talking part didn't last as long today.

For my final meditative session, we both placed ourselves in a place of peace, and then he began. Both his hands touched my shoulders and a wave of energy went through my body. With my eyes closed I began to see images, almost like how we do when we dream.

When he touched the top of my head, I saw a great white dragon. Her eyes were the color of honey and her mane was blue. I saw the Egyptian pyramids, the all-seeing eye of the dragon coming closer and closer towards me.

John began his guided meditation. He led me into a lush green forest.

"You look up and see the bright blue sky. The sun shines warmly on your skin. You can hear birds chirping and fluttering amongst the trees. Butterflies float past you as you walk barefoot on the leaves and dirt. You begin to hear calm waves in the distance as the forest opens to a white sand beach. You notice a softness under your feet as the dirt slowly becomes sand."

In this vision of the beach, I saw a small group of people laughing and having fun together. They noticed me and all turned at once. A small Asian child ran to me and hugged my legs. The child grabbed my hand and walked me to their circle. An older white man with a thick beard and mustache, a middle-aged black woman adorned in beautiful African garb, a teenage black boy, an Indian woman. They all made room for me to sit.

We all sat and watched the sunset in silence. It was the largest I'd ever seen the sun, and the clouds were painted by colors as potent as those of a nebula. One by one the stars appeared, and the others set up a camp fire. When it was lit, we gathered around it like old friends. We laughed, talked, and enjoyed.

Time shifted and my mind traveled to other places. Eventually my mind cleared and I simply saw an empty white space. There was only silence.

"What do I do now?" I thought.
I heard a response from my Higher Self, "Just wait. Be patient."
So, I did.

I stopped looking for an outcome or trying to "do" something. Soon after, affirmations came to me.

I will live a life of Peace.
I will live a life of Love.
I will live life as a Healer.

When they finished, I was back at the beach with the group. It was very dark now and I told them it was time for me to go. I waved goodbye and walked up the beach and back into the forest. I journeyed through the trees and came to a blank, black space with a shadow. I opened my eyes.

John had interesting things to say about my visions. For the pyramid, he intuits that I was ranked high in those times. He sees that I was one of the female guards of the throne. Strong in my feminine, protecting, overseeing.

He says the dragon was cool because he saw her too. She came up next to him and said "I want her to be a part of me." He also suggested a book that I should read about her, called The Sophia Code.

He believes the people at the beach are my past selves. He says it's good that they were happy to see me and were congratulating me. Once, he led a client into the same meditation and the people at the beach were screaming and yelling at her.

The shadow part was a little confusing. He said it could be something of the past, a childhood trauma that I'm not ready to deal with. But it comes in peace and will show itself when its time.

I recognize that to some people these visions may sound "crazy" or "weird", but to me they are simply an extension of dreams. Some people interpret their dreams, some people forget them, some people never think about their dreams at all. But we all have the power to tap into our dreams, and they often contain powerful messages for us if we're open to listen.

Anthem 42

October 7th

I planned two events for my birthday this year. The first was a four-day trip to Banff, Canada with my best friends from college. The trip was so restorative, so enlivening, so honest and love-filled. I'm glad we planned and actually went through with the trip because, man, I needed it.

We saw elk and woodpeckers, climbed mountains, hiked at night into level four darkness. We saw the galaxy clear as day, spotted StarLink, caught views from a gondola, canoed on the most scenic Lake Louise, ran naked through a hotel hallway at 3am, flirted with cute bartenders, and created countless memories with my girls.

We were also able to reconnect with each other. We spoke of the trials we currently face, the grievances of our friendships, what we love about one another, key moments of each individual friendship, and sharing what we feel like each of us *needs* to hear.

We don't get to get together often, so it was truly grounding for me, and they left me a lot to think about. Each of them shared with me what they felt like I needed to hear.

Follow your intuition. What you feel is real.
Your words and actions affect people. Be careful with this power.
Plant love where it can grow. Love has to grow.

These words ring in my ears and vibrate my feels.

The next week I planned a birthday party with my family in South Carolina. My mom, gram and siblings all flew down from Chicago to celebrate. My dad invited all my cousins, nieces, and nephews to eat, sing, dance, and enjoy one another.

For my birthday I always take the time to do my 'birthday reflections'. I ask myself the same series of questions every single year. This helps to see where I've grown, where I may have stumbled, and remind me of all that I have to be grateful for.

The questions are:

- What were your favorite memories from this past year?

- Who really made this year special for you? Why? (thank them)

- What accomplishment(s) are you most proud of?

- What did you learn this year that you'd like to carry with you into the next?

- What was your MOST impactful life lesson?

- What habits or behaviors would you like to cultivate more of in this next year?

- What goals do you want to achieve this year?

I'm excited to start this new year. My twenties have been so full of growth, adventure, love, loss, joy, play, travel, friends, sex, cupcakes, sunlight, bare feet, hair changes, nudity, pain, and pleasure. The next year will bring abundance, prosperity, peace, love, new ventures, and continued growth. I speak life unto this and so it shall be.

Anthem 43

Sometimes I feel the weight of my past.
My unending insecurities.
My immense lack of self-worth.
My desire to feel loved, seen, accepted, and understood.

I know its these bags I carry that keep me from writing, that keep me from fully pursuing my sacred work. I'm afraid of being seen and yet still misunderstood.

That's why it's easier for me to post on TikTok, where I have 53 followers, than on Instagram where I have 15 thousand. It's why I was able to break all those records and set a new personal best at my first World Championship, when I was still unknown and had no expectations.

Do I crumble under the weight of expectation?

It's been the looming thought throughout my offseason. I always ask myself; do I really have what it takes?

Anthem 44

I began my day on the ground, staring blankly at the ceiling. I knew that below this seemingly innocent endeavor was a cloud that would not allow me to do anything else.

So there I lay. Unbathed. Unfed. No thoughts.

I kept the thoughts away because I knew what would come with them. Tears. Negative self-talk. Depression.

I instead repeated, "Get Up."

Get up and do something. Get up and clean yourself. Get up and feed yourself. Get up and find a way to feed your spirit.

After many attempts, I managed to get in the shower.

"Water is healing."

I turned the dial as far as it'd go. The steam filled the room and drops pricked at my skin like tiny scorched needles. I focused only on the feeling. I focused on the present sensation to stop my mind that was on the verge of a negative spiral. I closed my eyes and felt the warmth of water surrounding my toes. I turned as it drenched my back like a full body hug.

Michael Jackson's voice popped into my head and I began to sing. "You are not aloooone. I am here with yoouu." I kept going, mumbling past the words I didn't know. The song flowed seamlessly into the next as Whitney Houston rang through my mind. "Hey baybay, don't give up! You've got to hold on to what you've gotttt.

Oooo baybe, don't give uppppp, you've got to keep on moving, don't stop, yeea yeaa yeaaaaa!"

My spirits lifted, but I knew I needed to do more. I needed to keep taking care of me.

I got dressed, put on some lipstick and got on my bike. After a quick trip to the store for some kombucha and pickles (both good for womb healing) I rode to the Arboretum. Surrounded by trees, swept by the breeze, I immediately felt at peace. I listened to the chirp of the birds and the cackle of chipmunks. The sun shined brightly on me.

There are days when I feel on top of the world and even fathom to think that I no longer have "mental wellness issues." I forget that this is an ongoing journey, something I'll probably have to stay on top of for the rest of my life, especially during the change of seasons.

I'm proud of myself for recognizing what my spirit needed. I could still be lying on my carpet, staring at the ceiling, but I'm not. I chose differently. I chose better for myself because I'm finally in a place where I know without a doubt that I deserve better. So, I act accordingly.

I will always need the Sun, but I'll never again forget that I too am the Light.

With all the love I am,
Mee

Anthem 45

I'm reading the book John suggested for me, *The Sophia Code: A Living Transmission from the Sophia Dragon Tribe*. The book explores the lives of seven amazing women. It talks about all that these women accomplished in their human lives and then how that wisdom has perpetuated into the spirit realm, or "afterlife". It's all a bit 'out there', but in one particular chapter the book describes a number of "angels" that can come to us to provide us with faith, trust, clarity, alignment, anointing, atonement, grace and completion. These angels turn out to really be deeper aspects of our Higher Selves, and each section ends with a meditation so that you can better access the wisdom and guidance of the angels.

I listened to the first four or five chapters of the book with an open mind, but I hadn't really bought in. Eventually I came to one of the meditation sessions and decided I would try it. I verbally agreed to open myself to the experience, casually repeating some of the passages from the book. I went on Youtube and played a sound healing tone at a frequency that encourages healing and manifestation. I listened to the music and quieted all the random thoughts that popped up. The idea came to me to say one of the mantras I'd learned from the book, so I silently repeated it in my head.

Soon my body began to tingle. My feet, legs, arms, and hands all vibrated. In my mind I was elsewhere, out in space it seemed. I continued to repeat the mantra in my mind. A bright golden light appeared off in the distance. Intuitively, I switched from the mantra to humming "Om" out loud to the tune of the music. Energy rippled throughout my body. An image came from the bright light. A man of deeper complexion with long, full brown hair. At first, I thought it was Jesus, but as the man came closer, I recognized him as the angel of trust that the book describes.

This angel releases fear in the pursuit of one's purpose. He releases self-doubt, and he releases the fear of inadequacy. He emboldens you to trust in your own intuition, to trust your ability to know what is trustworthy, and to trust in your faith.

Once in front of me the man placed his hands on my shoulders. He was so close I could rest my head upon his chest. Tears welled up inside of me as he placed his hand over my heart. I began to cry. I could physically feel his presence, the warmth, the pressure, the safety, the trust. The music stopped and I was slowly coming back to my body, but his presence remained.

He whispered to me, "it's okay."

I nodded and then he left.

I opened my eyes to my living room. I didn't expect the angels to come so soon.

It was amazing.

Anthem 46

December 31, 2021

I'm not making hard goals and plans this year. God always has her own anyways. But I will manifest abundance, life, love, and positivity into all of my thoughts and actions. I will keep my heart and mind wide open for opportunity. I will listen to my intuition when it tells me to do or not to do something. I will allow myself to be creative and thrive on the art spewing from my soul. I will be me in my truest form, letting go of the illusion of self and begin my becoming.

Happy New Year.
With Love,
Mee

Anthem 47

My word for 2022 is WILL.

"Expressing the future tense.
Expressing inevitable events."

When I'm talking about a task that I will complete
or in regards to my ability to achieve,
It is simple.
It is done.
I WILL.

If it is God's will.
So it shall be.

Anthem 48

Sunflowers, orchids, and white roses are my favorite flowers. I see sunflowers as tall, strong, vibrant, and beautiful… the sun in plant form. I drove past a vast field of them today, but every single one was browned and wilted. I watched in dismay as flower after flower passed me by, all of them dead or dying. My gut tightened and my face twisted in discomfort.

I know all flowers must die. I think there is beauty in the death of a flower. It's why I've always loved potpourri. The scent is still potent, but the crumbled browned dullness of the flowers' once exquisite existence adds a realness to it. Even in their end, flowers can still influence life with their legacy.

But I've never considered what a sunflower would look like in its death. I'm not sure I would keep a sunflower once it's gone.

That makes me think of love, of course. Unconditional love. There are some things we will love through anything. All the good and the bad, the beauty and ugly, through life and death. While there are some things or people that we won't, like the sunflower in my case.

It begs the questions, what are some things that I will love through and through? What are some things or people that I wouldn't?

Maybe I wouldn't want to be around certain people if they weren't as they are now. And this question falls back on me too. I know there are people that wouldn't love me if I weren't as vibrant as I typically am. That actually used to be a huge fear of mine growing up. I never wanted anyone to know how depressed I was, or the sadness that loomed day in and day out. I wanted to be the laughter and joy in people's lives. I didn't want to disrupt their view of me.

I've since expanded beyond this thought process. I know there are people that haven't, don't, can't, or won't love me through my ups and downs. And that's okay. They don't need to, because I already know that I am not only loveable but that I am Love itself. I do not need to seek from any external source. Those that choose to love me through it all, will, and I will do the same for them.

I think it's okay that I don't feel the call to love a sunflower in its disarray. It is still loved, even if not by me. And I still feel a connection to it. I'll just leave that loving for someone who resonates more closely with it, as I'd hope someone would do for me.

Love doesn't need to be forced. Love flows freely and openly when in alignment.

Anthem 49

This morning I woke up at 7:35am, totally exhausted. I grabbed Leo, my teddy bear, and we began our morning meditation.

It consisted mostly of focused breathing. I tried to fill my entire lower belly, then slowly fill more air up toward my sternum, and upper chest. Filling my stomach and upper chest has gotten pretty easy for me, but my solar plexus area, just below my sternum, is still a struggle. However, today I started to feel it more.

The solar plexus focuses on confidence and self-esteem. Two things that I was completely lacking in 2021. I can sense this changing though. Belief in myself and my abilities is coming back to me now. On the track I'm starting to feel that fire that comes with confidence.

True confidence, not just me saying "I can do it" to mask my underlying fear of failure.

I asked God and the guardians to guide me closer to my Higher Self, to help hear and feel my inner voice so that I may live more fully and honestly. I'm seeking to listen to my intuition more.

They respond to me. "To seek your Higher Self is a fruitless task. To seek your Higher Self is like swimming in the ocean looking for water."

I AM my Higher Self.

I should instead be working on quieting my Ego. Silencing the voices that want to 'fit in', have more money, live 'the lifestyle' of influencers or Hollywood celebrities. I'm the only one in the way of having a deeper connection to the great I AM.

My meditation ended by sending love, compassion, understanding, and healing unto the world. I visualized a pure white energy flowing from all around me like a sheer silk blanket, spreading throughout my apartment, filling my neighbor's home, then all of Ann Arbor. I watched the light engulf Michigan and make its way to Chicago. It covered my mother, brothers, and grandmother in their sleep, then continued to spread throughout the states.

I breathed deeply into this healing that I sent. I placed my hand firmly over my heart, and I breathed open my heart chakra.

"I open my chakras. I unlock the broken imbalances that keep them clenched and scared. I allow them to release and flow seamlessly from my root to my crown. I send myself love, peace, self-acceptance and healing."

I opened my eyes and kissed little Leo, who sat just before me.

It's now 8 something and I'll start some light movement because my body is sore from lift yesterday. Then I'll make breakfast and write. I like this early morning routine. I think I'll continue it.

Smooches,
Mee

Anthem 50

I went to an acupuncture appointment yesterday to see if she could do something about the pain I was feeling in my knees. I've gone to her a few times, knowing that she's familiar with energy meridians and constitutions. I was hoping she could get down to the bottom of this knee and back pain. We talked a lot, did the treatment, and at the end she told me that I was holding a lot of heat in the solar plexus area, right at the bottom of my sternum. She said that energy was being blocked there.

I went home trying not to be disappointed by the fact that my knee was still hurting, when I received a call from a friend about a conversation he had with a different acupuncturist I saw a couple months ago. This acupuncturist believes that my blockage is in my liver meridian, and from what he recalls, it seems I have repressed anger. Figures.

My friend encouraged me to try a screaming exercise. It's probably true that I have repressed anger; I have many past experiences that I could be angry about. But I don't want to be angry. It doesn't serve me, nor does it solve anything. Naturally I was hesitant, but later that evening I did it anyways.

I crawled in my bed, placed two foam pillows over my face, and *screamed*. At first, I wasn't thinking or screaming about anything specific. I just screamed, and I kept screaming until eventually my old coach's face came into view. I screamed at him, right into his face. I gathered it from the deepest parts of my lungs and howled at him with all my rage. I screamed for being back in Michigan and all the feelings being back here made me have. The lack of sun. Lack of friends. Lack of diversity. I yelled at all the boys or men that touched me or crossed my boundaries. I screamed at the embarrassment of failing so horribly in Tokyo. I yelled at the white boy that called me a n***er in elementary school, the white kids that excluded me or made me feel weird or different. I screamed for the families of those whose lives are lost to gun violence, I screamed at feeling hopeless against police brutality. I screamed at my feelings of abandonment. I screamed at it all and then I screamed some more, until eventually my screams turned to tears.

I allowed the tears to release. The pillow still pressed to my face, the muffled cries shook my body until every face or memory quietly disappeared.

When my body stopped trembling, I placed one hand over my heart and the other over my womb. I meditated, breathing, feeling the stillness of my room and my thoughts. I reminded myself that I am protected, I am loved, and that I am safe.

Anthem 51

2/2/22

They say today is the day of connection and opportunity. Apparently, you can manifest whatever you want on this day.

So here goes.

> I am manifesting consistent legal triple jumps over 14.50s for the rest of 2022.

> I am manifesting mental, emotional, and physical health.

> I am manifesting that my menstrual cycle will normalize.

> I am manifesting peace within myself and acceptance of all that life is.

> I am manifesting a six-figure income for 2022.

> I am manifesting that my plants will flourish.

> I am manifesting that You Anthem will be published in spring 2022.

> I am manifesting love to be felt by all those who encounter me.

I love you,
Mee

Anthem 52

I decided I'm going to allow myself to be more grateful. It's obvious Michigan isn't my first choice of a place to live; for some reason I can't get away from the cold. But if I continue to resist where I am, my mind and spirit will not be open to what this chapter of my life has to teach me. It will stunt my growth if I can't be open to receive.

When I think about or fantasize about my future, I always skip ahead to the life I envision in Costa Rica. I think of all the retreats I want to host all over the world. I never think about or get excited about the present or near future. I still have a few more years in this sport, and I'm never thinking about it. What do I plan for my life in the semi-short term? What growth do I hope to experience NOW?

I vow to bring more openness, love, and gratefulness into my spirit. The universe has plans for me. I can feel it. I won't step in my own way.

Anthem 53

This morning I woke up a little earlier than normal because I had a Reiki client. I lit some incense, began the healing tunes, and waited. My client never showed. But since I hadn't done my meditation for the morning and the scene was already set, I decided to meditate and reiki myself.

I began with a simple meditation of power. I began from my feet, saying, "My feet are powerful."

I moved up.
"My ankles are powerful."

I ascended through my body, naming each part of it. Giving, realizing, and opening the power in every corner of my body.

I continued with supporting statements like:
My body is light and quick. My body can handle immense amounts of force. My body can *emit* immense amounts of force. I went back to my "I am powerful" statements and sat in it.

I then visualized myself triple jumping. Fast, strong, powerful, and technically sound.

When I finished, I placed my hands on my womb. My womb has been on its menses for seven weeks. I have been bleeding for seven straight weeks. A part of me just accepted this new reality, that this is how my body is going to operate from now on.

The other day I watched a documentary called 'Heal'. It reminded me that healing isn't just something you do for others when asked, but something you do for yourself when needed. I forgot that I can physically heal myself too. My womb keeps bleeding because I've accepted that it will.

I'm no longer accepting this as a reality. I will balance my womb.

I laid down and put both hands on my womb, allowing the reiki energy to take hold. Tingles shot through my fingers as I asked God to help balance the hormones and regulate my menses. I told my womb to clear out whatever was left and begin the new cycle. Stop the bleeding and prepare for the new egg.

When this was finished, I moved my left hand to my heart, and almost immediately my eyes began to tear. I wasn't sad, I felt love. I just felt love.

I was called to place both hands on my third eye. My palms tingled over my closed eyelids. I was spoken to. Source told me that I had to let go in order for the power to connect. I breathed there for a while. Then I asked, 'how can I connect deeper with you?'

And Source said, 'You ARE.'

Then it was like my spirit was shooting through space. Stars whizzed past me, and my body was stretched to twice its size. It felt as if the air I was breathing was more pure, and my body became lighter. The stars surrounded me and an aura presented itself. Flowing before me, I could see all the colors of the Universe.

I was overwhelmed with gratitude. That was the only word replaying in my mind.

Gratitude.
Gratitude.
Gratitude.

Love and emotion filled my eyes, and I gently cried. I breathed and sat in the presence of this loving, powerful, understanding Aura.

Beauty is an understatement.
Then the Aura was gone.

I removed my hands from my third eye and allowed the rest of the tears to flow. I stretched my body and smiled.

I feel content. Safe. Ok with everything. I have not a single worry. I am connected.

With All the Love I AM,
Mee

Anthem 54

Tomorrow I jump in my sixth indoor national championship. I'm feeling pretty chill. Not stressing or anything. I'm just ready to go compete. I'm in Spokane Washington in an Airbnb by myself. I haven't spoken to nor seen anyone really. My mom and grandma came to watch me. I love that they come to watch me jump so often. It means so much to me. Their support keeps me going and lets me know that I'm not out here doing this alone. I love them for that.

Anthem 55

A few weeks ago, I competed at the USA Indoor National Championships, where I qualified for my fourth Indoor World Championships. I didn't jump well or anything, but it got me all the way to Belgrade, Serbia to represent the United States. I came in with the hope of jumping well. I believed that I could medal if everything came together. I believe that one day in the future I will medal, multiple times. But I was also very aware of how I've been jumping all season. High 13 meters. Which, for the record, is *terrible* by my standards. If I happen to jump something similar here in Serbia, I won't be surprised. It would make sense.

And so, I did. I jumped 13.85m. Thirteenth place, missing finals. I didn't shed a single tear. I didn't really have any emotional response. Mostly because, as I said, I haven't jumped 14 meters all season. I haven't felt fast nor powerful.

Since competing I've talked to my mom and gram, some old training partners from France, a couple coaches from Greece, and they've all said the same thing.

"You are a completely different jumper."
"It's like you have no power."
"Your run is too, 'Bam bam bam!' Too heavy!"
"You look like you did when you came right out of college."

My agent called me and said that she doesn't think this training is working for me. "If this season doesn't go well, you won't have a sponsor next year."

It's do or die.

I had lunch with my mom and grandma, who flew all the way to Serbia for the weekend just to watch me compete. Before I mentioned anything, they said that I needed to try a different training situation. I listened quietly as they stated their reasons why, and when they finished, I simply said, "I agree."

Later that evening, I went to find a friend of mine, Tasos. He's a youth coach and very good friends with the coach that I wished to work with. Tasos told me that he and Giorgos Pomaski would be watching the competition together and that I was welcome to join.

I was nervous but excited. I knew there was a real possibility that he would say no...again. Almost exactly one year ago, I asked him to coach me after I was kicked out of my training group in Paris. He told me no, because he said it would be too much to try to organize with so little time before the Tokyo Olympics. He said I'd be better off going to a situation that I know and can feel comfortable in. He'd also said that if I wanted to come in the fall I could, but when the season ended last year I was just so mentally defeated and energetically exhausted that I didn't have it in me to organize a cross-Atlantic move again. So, I stayed in Michigan and hoped for the best.

Pomaski is a Bulgarian man in his mid-sixties, with a tall, broad frame, shaggy hair, and youthful eyes. He smiles and jokes a lot, but most of it I can never understand because he doesn't speak much English. Yet, any other Slavic language he speaks with ease.

Tasos opened the door to their booth and welcomed me with a hug. I put down my coat and bag and found a spot between him and Pomaski. Tasos brought me a beer (I don't like beer, so I barely sipped on it), and we watched the races in front of us. Slowly, chatter about my competition began. Pomaski asked what I've been doing in training. I just explained where I was, how I'd been training, why I think I've competed the way I did. I went on to say that I know his training style, I've seen how he coaches his athletes for years, and I need to be with a coach whose methods I trust.

Again, he was hesitant. "World Championships is again this summer. I don't know how quick you can make the changes."

"I can make the changes. I can do it."
"Hmm.."
Pomaski took a sip of his beer and stared out onto the track, as if pondering the meaning of life.

"You need 100% focus. We go very strong."
I nodded.
"Are you ready for this," he asked in his thick Bulgarian accent.
"I'm ready," I said assuredly. "I can do this."
We shook hands and I smiled, adding a well-needed, "yaaayyyy!"

In 10 days, I'm moving to Greece.

Athens, Greece

Anthem 56

April 3rd 2022

I'm on the tail end of my long flight to Istanbul, Turkey, and it looks like I'm going to miss my connecting flight to Athens. I texted mama to see if she can rebook my flight to Athens before I land. My only worry is that my luggage will get lost in the hustle and bustle. I'm not super worried about it at the moment, but it would definitely be an inconvenience.

The last week and a half has been crazy busy, but everything I planned went off without a hitch. My final days in Ann Arbor were full of packing, training, last-minute doctors' appointments, and quick goodbyes.

Most people just received text messages that I was leaving. Some wanted to meet up, but I just didn't have the time. But I did get to finally have an Olympic celebration/goodbye dinner with Coach Sterls, his wife, my training partner Donald, and my mom, who drove over from Chicago to help me move.

The evening was full of stories and laughter. I'm going to miss our little team. My coach almost made me cry earlier in the week when we said our goodbyes. He said that he just hopes that I find the home I'm looking for, that I find somewhere that I can be truly happy, and it sucks that it wasn't there.

Emotionally, it's a lot to move back out of the country to follow this dream. Having to pack up my entire life again. Always living out of a suitcase gets a little old sometimes. I was really wrapping my head around living in Ann Arbor for the next two years. Making business plans and creating ideas for my non-profit. Now it seems like my future is all up in the air again. But all I can do is focus on these moments right now.

My mom and I drove back to Chicago the morning after the dinner to leave *more* boxes and bags in her garage. I wouldn't have finished packing in time if she hadn't come. I was going to start freaking out, and she just dropped everything and drove to Michigan. She's my rock. I know she'd do anything for me, and she *always* follows through. I want to be that kind of mother one day.

I put my apartment up for sublease the day after I got back from Serbia. I found a subletter three days later who was ready to move in the day I left. Yesterday Tasos messaged me and said that he found a studio apartment for me in Athens for a good price. I have a place to live when I land! The ease of these two events shows me that this is in alignment. When things fall into place like this, it means the Universe supports the journey.

I won't be going to my "new" studio when I arrive. One of my new training partners will pick me up from the airport and drive us two and a half hours to a town called Kalamata for training camp. I'll be hitting the ground running. I've been there before; it's right by the beach. I plan to dip in the water, bask in the sun, and get back to my state of peace and love.

Anthem 57

I've finished two weeks of my three-week training camp in Kalamata. This shouldn't be a surprise, but the olives here are impeccable. Training, in short, is going extremely well. My running has improved. The way my foot contacts the track is smoother and more precise. My marks are continually improving. And I have complete confidence in my coach. He has expressed excitement and good juju for the season as well, which makes me feel confident and happy overall.

I've felt really happy. The sun has been charging my spirit. My skin is healing, my hair is locking, and I feel like I'm exactly where I need to be.

The training group is also cool. I think because I knew some of them before coming it was easier to integrate into the group. Everyone is nice, and I'm slowly building individual relationships with each person.

The last two Saturdays I've gone to the beach in search of something beautiful. I sat on the small pebbles gazing out at the Mediterranean Sea. The sun glistened amongst the ripples.

"I'm on a beach in Greece," I thought to myself.

Two weeks ago I was living in Michigan, and now I'm all the way across the world feeling better than I have in months. I love that my life is so spontaneous. I've gone on adventures that I couldn't have planned myself. Sometimes I think destiny plays a bigger role in things than people think. It feels like the last five years have all been preparing me to live in Greece, training under this coach.

In 2016 I was on an airplane flying to compete at the Olympic Trials. I sat next to a chatty man I'd later know as Mark. I told him that I was thinking about leaving my university, and he suggested a coach in my hometown, Chicago. Mark called Andreas Pavlou there on the spot, just as we were lifting off, and we set up a time to talk when I returned home. For the next two years I worked with Coach Andy in Chicago. Together we got me to my first World Championships, my first 14-meter jump, my first Diamond Leagues, and two American Records together. We also spent our summers at his home in Athens, Greece, where I first met Pomaski. Every year we went I became more comfortable with the extended stays abroad. I developed more understanding of the Greek culture, grew more interested in the language, and became more connected with the other athletes and coaches.

I eventually left that coach and stopped going to Athens, but in my heart I always knew I'd return at some point. I thought it would be for vacation or something… who knew it would be to live for the next few years!

The relationship I built with Tasos and Pomaski during that period is the only reason I am able to be here now. It was all preparing me for this time of my life. And in some way that I cannot yet foresee, this is preparing me for another time in my life yet to come. It really is all connected.

I say it's destiny, but really, it's my philosophy that destiny is created by the decisions we make. Every choice we make leads us to the exact conclusion that we were meant to experience. There is no such thing as a good choice or a bad choice; every choice was made with intention. If the result of that intention is a positive experience, amazing! If the result is a negative experience, then that's exactly what you were meant to experience. It was meant to teach you, to help you grow, to incur some suffering so that you will make some mental, emotional, spiritual, or physical change in your life. There are no bad decisions, only *decisions,* and where we end up was our destiny all along.

I wasn't supposed to do well in Tokyo. I was *supposed* to be in Michigan during the time that I was there. I wasn't ready to compete well in Serbia because I wasn't meant to… I needed to do badly there so that I would be thrust into this major life change. I'm on the right path. We all are. It's just a matter of recognizing that and understanding what this part of your life is trying to teach you.

With Love,
Mee

Anthem 58

I've been called crazy my entire life. I know most of the time people mean a 'good' type of crazy. And for the most part I think I'd agree with them. What kind of person continues to pursue something after countless failures? A crazy one. Someone who loses more than they win but keeps going has to be at least a little crazy. The type of person to travel across the world not once but twice, for a goal that could very well continue to fail. Crazy. Someone who will jump on the back of a stranger's motorcycle just to get to a date on time, trespass over a fence to see a nice view, almost jump out of a three-story window to practice her new fire escape techniques, travel the world alone, chase a general manager down the street and hound him for an interview even though she had zero experience (and get the job by the way), eat hints of peanut butter to build an 'immunity' to her allergy, dance wherever and whenever regardless of who is around, eat seven cupcakes in two days, scream at the top of her lungs on a hill, in the car, underwater, into a pillow. Or fall in love over and over again because she believes in love after love.

All of these can arguably be considered a good, all be it risky, Crazy. Yet sometimes, I don't feel crazy in the positive light. I just feel...crazy... like something is wrong with me.

IS something wrong with me?

Anthem 59

A Letter from My Brother Brandon

So, I actually do think you are crazy, but like you said, in a good way. The type of crazy that makes you a world-class athlete. You have to be crazy to try to achieve the unachievable. Only crazy people continue to do something after failing, and that's why they reach further than others. I also don't think you're "too masculine." I think you are assertive and at times aggressive, but that's because you've had to be to get where you are today. Just find balance, you are a black woman from a tough city raised by strong, tough women. You haven't had the privilege to be soft or weak, but in life we grow and find balance where needed.

I haven't had the privilege of being soft. I haven't had the privilege of having things handed to me or done for me. I haven't been able to show emotion or whine or crumble. I know I write about all these feelings, but that hasn't always been how I've carried myself in the world. There is no space for weakness for a black woman living in America.

But I don't want to be strong anymore. I don't want to have to have it all together and always watch my own back and take care of everything. I don't want to pretend like it doesn't hurt. I want to be able to relax, feel, cry, have needs. I want to ask for reassurance and let my guard down. Maybe I want help and guidance to handle it all. I want to let go of survival mode and just live. I want to feel safe enough to FEEL, to connect, to let go.

Anthem 60

This morning I asked the question, "How come every time I get to where I need to be (in my fitness/triple jumping), something happens and it knocks me back down?"

When I was in France I had a great few weeks of training at a camp in Clermont-Ferrand, then as soon as we got back to Paris mice invaded my apartment and ruined my entire mental state. During the training camp in Kalamata, I was picking up everything so quickly and literally making leaps and bounds of improvement. Then my knee started acting up, slowing down my progress. Last Wednesday, I triple jumped for the first time in eight weeks, and I jumped 13.64m from eight steps. It was glorious. Then four days later my hamstring decided to tighten up and send me into disarray.

Why is it then? When I begin to taste success, something sabotages it. My theory: I subconsciously am not prepared to accept my destiny of success. Maybe I look for things to go wrong so that if I were to fail, I'd have an excuse. Maybe I'm afraid of what comes with success. If I succeed, will I be able to maintain it? There would be a new pressure to continue to do well. Maybe I'm afraid of that pressure. Subconsciously I am attracting the energy of fear and failure, so that when the tiniest thing goes wrong, it becomes something that dismantles my success. That's the theory anyway.

After acknowledging this possibility, I've decided to REBUKE the Devil! I am done sabotaging and being fearful. I will compete to my full potential. I have trained hard. I've moved out the country, again! And I can be consistent, I can handle the pressure, the attention, everything. I am ready for my success story! I am more focused than I've ever been, and after thirteen years I finally understand what the triple jump is and how to do it.

I don't need my college alter ego, ToTo. I don't need anger and aggression. I don't need music. I don't need a crowd. I can do it anywhere, anytime, because I know what the fuck I'm capable of.

This morning I woke up with my hamstring/popliteus hurting. I brought my cups to practice and did treatment. I warmed up until I was dripping, and I did what my coach asked of me. I don't usually lift the day before a competition, but I trust him. By the end of practice my pain was gone. I'm ready to jump far tomorrow. I can feel it.

The door to all your dreams is open. It's up to you to walk through it. As for me, I'm *running* through!

Anthem 61

I opened my season with a season opener personal best… it's the farthest I've ever jumped in a first competition, and it came so easily! I honestly just had fun and did exactly as I've been training. No overexertion or trying too hard, no stress or pressure. I just leaped, gracefully and playfully.

I know this season will be different than I've ever experienced.

Anthem 62

I remember the first time I came to Athens with Coach Andy in 2017. There was something about it that didn't sit well with me. The buildings are old and covered in graffiti; some of its very beautiful artistry, but most is just chicken scratch.

There are many tourists and tons of traffic in the city center. The suburbs are lined with aged apartment buildings with balconies and shades to keep the heat out. They're not exactly aesthetically pleasing.

The city just wasn't what I was expecting. Then I realized... the only image that I had in my mind of Greece came from two sources. Hercules, the Disney channel movie, and photos of Mykonos. Athens looks like neither.

Hercules is obviously a cartoon set in ancient Greek times. How could I expect a modern city to be filled with horse carriages and shiny marble columns everywhere? I let go of this delusion, and as my time here became more frequent, I learned to love Athens for what it is.

I like that there is graffiti everywhere. It's scrappy, tells a story, and shows that the people of Athens are done with the old and run down. I love the tight, narrow streets of Psyri, the dive bars in Exarcheia, drinks in Kolonaki, dancing in Gazi. I like eating at the local taverna in Galatsi where the souvlaki, kolokythokeftedes, and saganaki are amazing. I like exploring and finding beautiful views of the entire city, like Anafiotika and Lycabettus Hill. Or escaping the hustle and bustle by going south to Vouliagmeni or Sounion, where the water is crisp, clear, and always so welcoming.

Of course, everyone loves the Greek islands. But Athens has its own allure, and I've learned to appreciate the city's sun, fresh food, and beauty just as it is.

Anthem 63

<u>New Moon Intentions</u>

I will be 100% healthy for both USA Nationals 2022 and World Championships 2022
I will make all decisions with training as the priority
I will get my weight down to 56kg for the World Championship
I will remain focused
I will continue/start writing more
I will grow more in tune with my body
I will grow more connected to the Divine Life Source
I will open my heart and mind to the omens of the Universe
I will be brave
I am at ease
I accept all of life's successes that are meant for me
I deserve and am worthy of success

With Love,
Mee

Anthem 64

I've figured out a way to listen to my old music on my phone. The song *My Own Fault,* by Manny Walters, came on and I got the feeling of nostalgia. Have you ever listened to an old song that used to really mean something to you? A song you replayed over and over? I listen to it and realize how different I am now than I was five years ago. I'm the same in all the best ways, but I'm different in all the meaningful ones.

I just feel gratitude. Gratitude for growth. I'm proud to have gotten through those times, for carrying myself through and into many new and continuously unfolding chapters of my life.

I hear this song and I remember blasting it in my hotel room before Mt. Sac, a competition in Walnut, California. The theme of the hotel was a sailor's ship. There were pictures of sailboats hanging on the light blue walls. Thick rope lined the decorative mirrors and there was a tall, white floor lamp with a half dome frame that directed the light. I twisted the flexible neck to face me like a spot light. I grabbed Leo, my teddy bear, who doubled as my microphone and dance partner. We stood on the crisp, white sheets of the bed, and together we sang to the smooth raspy tune of Manny Walters. Over and over, we sang.

I yearned for connection. I was always lonely. I loved those who did not love me.

I remember that version of me. I feel reassured in a sense, because I can look back at where I was and be proud of <u>her</u>, in all her mess, and feel content and at peace with where I am now. The growth I've experienced only makes me look forward to my future more.

I imagine a 34-35 year old me, hearing *Rise* by Willow Smith (which I listen to all the time right now), and future me being proud of who I am now. Proud of the decisions I make. Proud of who and how I love. Proud of me for continuing to be my authentic self. Proud of what I accomplish in this period of my life. I imagine that this song, attached to the memories of now, will bring a sense of peace to her as well. I recognize in this moment that the things I'm going through or will soon experience are what will bring me to that future state of peace.

I'm proud of myself already.

Anthem 65

Did you know that trees can move? I don't mean like swaying in the breeze, but trees can travel from one location to another. They pick up their roots and very slowly shuffle their way to a place that better suits their needs. Branches and plants bend and reach to meet sunlight, but this is different.

Studies have also shown that plants hear and respond to music and the emotions given to them. Plants that are loved and sung to grow faster, stronger, and have more vibrant flowers. Others that feel negative energy in their environment wither away.

It sounds to me like plants are sentient. They can feel emotion and energy. They can bend and change shape to care for themselves. Would it be so farfetched to believe that they can walk? That they can travel and communicate amongst themselves?

Granted, I don't think every tree does this. Trees that have been planted in highly-populated areas don't move or speak much, I'd assume. My theory is that they don't know that they can. Most trees that you see planted in cities were grown on a farm. They were raised perfectly in row, snipped to the perfect shape, then sent off to some resort or concrete jungle. Any tree that didn't fit the perfect mold was cut down and made into a chair or trinkets, or sold at a truck stop in boo-foo nowhere.

These trees have forgotten what or who they are. They have lost connection to Nature, to the wild roots that came before them. They only know order, clippings, humans, roots that are confined to malnourished dirt that will stunt their growth. They are separate from each other. Standing alone, dividing the streets we drive. Roots cramming into cement. And every time a branch reaches in search of light, they are cut to keep their shape.

How sad that must be. To be a tree, capable of an array of emotion, capable of communicating through the cadence of their rustling leaves, to have once been a nomad in another life, and not know a thing of it. Confined to thick, cold, hard foundation unnatural to the Earth. Unable to grow, to speak, to move. Disconnected.

I believe one day they'll find their way back. When our time as rulers of this world is over, the trees will remain. They will wait patiently in the silence, and when they are sure all is clear, they will bust through the sidewalks. They will call to one another. They will stretch to the Sun and they will again walk freely. Connected once more, with roots as thick as the pipes they'll crush along the way. The wind will be filled with the sound of their rustling leaves as they sing and rejoice for miles upon miles.

Anthem 66

A couple days ago I competed at the U.S National championships. I felt so calm, at peace, free, and light. I was honestly nervous, but in a good way... the same way a child is when they are about to perform at a talent show or something.

I'd practiced this skill, this talent, for months. I kept it to myself, slaving away, doing my best to be a true student and perfect it. And then, it was finally time to show everyone. It was finally time to let the world see what I've worked on. The curtains were raised and there I was in the middle of the stage, ready to perform.

Boy, did I perform. I finished second with 14.59 meters. Forty-seven feet, ten inches. I fouled two jumps over 15 meters. It was an amazing day, and I was so close to making history again. I was pissed actually. I felt so deeply that I should've won, that the gold was supposed to be mine. My blood boiled when anyone told me congratulations. But I let it go. Nationals is merely a stepping stone. It is a means to an end, and the end is the World Championships in one month.

P.S My period has finally stopped and me weight is down to 57.5kg.

Anthem 67

Why ruin the silence? Why ruin the perfectly still, yet endlessly vibrating silence with your senseless words? Your questions that have no root or purpose other than to keep your mouth busy. Do you fear getting caught in the net of silence? Do you think we won't make it back? Will we sit in it a minute too long and cease to reconnect?

Silence shouldn't be something you run from, rather something you embrace when it comes. In silence you find out what's real. You notice the intricacies of the most subtle expressions and movements. You can see a soul in the depths of emptied sound. It shows you what it truly means to connect, to not force a time filler. Sound doesn't follow the same rules as time. In silence, you can live the same moment for ages.

You can spend eons in silence if you're able to glimpse the right soul. And that time is spent in bliss.

Anthem 68

Training camp in Seattle has been the bee's knees! Coach and the Greeks are here too. We all leave for Eugene, Oregon in one week!!

Today after my morning practice, as I walked back to my hotel room, I passed a feather the color of charcoal, perfectly placed in the middle of my path. I initially walked past it, but I remembered that in Native American (and many other) cultures feathers can have a symbolic message. I deduced that it was most likely a crow feather, judging by the copious number of crows in the area.

Crow feathers symbolize intuition and rebirth. Some Native Americans believe these feathers provide strength to face the unknown and bring about transformation.

I should mention that I have a crow tattoo on my neck. When I was younger, I developed an intense fear of crows. As I grew up, I challenged that fear by approaching crows when I saw them, and in doing so the fear subsided. I chose to get a crow tattoo as a reminder to face all of life's fears head-on. Not to erase fear, but to remember not to be afraid of fear itself.

I went back and collected the feather.

I continued my walk and decided to test my theory of that feather being a sign. So, I asked God, "Can I have another feather? I'd like another one."

Moments later, there was another beautiful feather along my path. It's kismet.

I've been jumping AMAZINGLY in practice. Ever since I began working with Pomaski we've done 4-alternate bounds a lot. When I first began with him, I was bounding 16.50 - 16.90 meters. It took a little over a month for me to break 17 meters. 17.25 and 17.61 meters happened at the end of May. It was right after my season-opening triple jump of 14.34 meters.

This afternoon in the 4-alternate bounds I jumped 18.20 meters and then 18.80 meters in training. TWO METERS further than I did a few months ago. It was freaking insane. And it came so easily… I floated! Even coach himself walked up to me and said, "I don't believe it. I don't believe you make so much improvement." His hands were nearly above his head, as if only God could explain it all.

Spyridoula, my training partner, said that while I was away, he was sending her my training videos that I'd sent him. She imitated him in her Greek-Bulgarian impression, "She is like demonized. So focused. She is a beast." We chuckled at his excitement and broken English.

I feel this excitement too, but I also feel extremely relaxed. In training I am very focused. Every movement is intentional. I can feel everything within my body and control it. From my toes to my hips, the erection of my spine, the sway of my arms and flow of my shoulders. The one thing I'm working on is my neck. It still gets a little stiff sometimes.

Yet, with all this connection I still notice when a bird flies overhead. I still take in the warmth of the sun. I am so much more present.

I barely think, if at all. I just feel.

I've received a lot of messages from the spirit world/universe lately. I see 444 almost every day. I've also seen 333 the last few days. The angel number 444 means that the angels have you covered. All of your ambitions and future goals are already taken care of. Any worry or doubt about them can be released. You don't need to spend any extra energy being afraid.

What I have been working so hard toward is already written. It's a sign that change is on the horizon.

The angel number 333 says that your guardian angel is there to provide strength and the ability to take one step at a time while I live a stress-free life.

I saw this number while I was trying to figure out my rooming situation here in Seattle. I was under the assumption that Pomaski would organize a room for me at the university with the rest of the team during training camp. When they arrived, I checked out of my hotel thinking I would move with them, but he said that the federation did not book a room for me. So I was scrambling trying to find somewhere to stay for the last few days of training.

Let me tell you, Seattle is not cheap! I had to leave my hotel, stay in an Airbnb for two nights, then switch to a hotel again. I spent close to $4000 for lodging. It's all taken care of now; I'll stay in this hotel for the rest of my stay. But seeing the angel numbers was a comforting sign.

I'm not worrying about the money because I attract money. It comes to me in abundance. My mind is set on Abundance, not lack.

Anthem 69

I've decided I'm going to compete in black nail polish and black lipstick.

There are two significant reasons for this. One, black is a color of mystique. It represents our highest potential. It allows us to connect to our deeper power and manifest our greatest desires. It is a color of authority, self-control, and transformative energy. Black absorbs, it is not easily overtaken, making it averse to negativity.

The second reason is in protest. It is in grieving. I am grieving for the country that I represent. A country that doesn't seem to care about the thousands of lives lost to mass shootings around the country almost daily. A country that protects pigs after they murder a black man with sixty bullet wounds. RIH George Floyd, Jay Walker, Sandra Bland and countless other names. A country where seemingly overnight, women no longer have control over our own bodies.

In what I do for a living, I've mastered the art of compartmentalizing. I can't think, worry, be stressed, upset, or sad about other things going on in my life or in the world. I have to focus. I have to be able to compete. But that doesn't mean that I don't feel the heavy, negative frequency of this country. So instead of "feeling" it in a time that is not optimal for me, I show it in black lipstick and black nail polish.

To feel it all would be too much. I would drown. It would deplete everything that I am to imagine how the parents of those lost children feel, to acknowledge the damage these countless murders do to the black community. We are all suffering, but we have to keep going. It would shatter me entirely to feel for the women who have been assaulted but are now forced to carry a child of rape.

By writing, by doing small things like lipstick and nail polish at a track meet, I can try to still be light in a dark world. I can still try to send positive energy into this low frequency place we call America the Great.

Anthem 70

Tomorrow I compete in the finals of the women's triple jump at the World Championships. I'm finally feeling ready and confident going into a World Championship meet. The prelims went well, but there are a couple things I want to fix in preparation for the final.

First and foremost, my first attempt will be a legal mark (as well as the next five, but very important to get the first one fair). Two competitions in a row I've fouled my first attempt, which has been one of my farthest jumps of the competition. That won't happen tomorrow.

Second, on my second attempt I collapsed from the 1st to the 2nd phase... my contact was a little in front of me. I will be more mindful of that.

Coach also wants me to do more running in my warmup, and less elastics, to make sure my body is open and free when I get on the runway. Sometimes I continue to get warmer during the competition, and then my run opens up more and I foul a lot because I'm running so much faster. So, I think it's a splendid idea to emphasize more running in my warmup.

I'm ready for this. I am ready to receive Abundance in my life. I am ready for success. I am fearless in all my pursuits. I am guided by angels who have told me all is ready for me. I can be free of worry. I can feel it in my bones. I am going to jump 15 meters tomorrow. Twice.

With love,
Mee

Anthem 71

July 19th

On the morning of every competition I do a shakeout, a light jog, and some stretching. The day of finals was no different. I went to a nearby field, took off my shoes (so I could feel the grass and practice grounding), listened to my music, and ran back and forth. The sun shined brightly on my face, sending warmth and love throughout my body. I danced to the upbeat music and warmed my body in preparation for the evening. When I finished I sat in the grass, faced the light, and meditated. I breathed my usual affirmations and filled my spirit with love, light, joy, and a sense of freedom. I opened my eyes, turned to grab my shoes, and there laying neatly with my things was a black crow feather.

I can't explain the feeling of peace that consumed me. It was as if God was sending me a personalized letter. "The work is done," I imagined it said. "You are ready. You have listened, you have trusted, and you have remained at peace. You can move forward fearlessly and with courage. Your mind, body, and spirit are finally in alignment. Now go out there and 'Play.'"

I took the feather. I passed a lavender bush while walking to the hotel and stopped to whiff the sweet, relaxing scent. I asked the bush if I could take a flower. I gently removed the lavender and gave thanks to the bush for this gift. I then tied the feather and the lavender together with a piece of long, browned grass.

During the competition, after three jumps, I sat in fourth place with a mark of 14.54 meter. I told myself to stop "trying" and just go do it. Do the things we've been working on in training. Run the run the way coach encourages and let it go. I've been telling myself its already written, so now is the moment to go all in.

I can let go and be free because the medal is already mine.

I relaxed my body and ran down the runway with all my speed. The hop came naturally. The step was effortless. And the jump soared with ease.

I solidified my spot in third. I am the first American woman to ever win a medal in the triple jump.

3rd place with 14.72 meters. 48 feet 3 inches, from well behind the board.

My first attempt was indeed a foul, and it was one of the two 15-meter jumps that I promised myself. For my final attempt, I gave everything I had in the quest for silver, but I fouled by two inches. The jump landed around the 15.20-meter mark. I jumped 15 meters twice. Not exactly what I was hoping for, but a prophecy come true nonetheless. I should be more specific about whether it's legal or not.

I am extremely grateful. I feel very proud of myself for getting to where I am today and an immense amount of peace about the journey forward.

After a competition like this I have 100% confidence that I can recreate these 14.70-15 meter jumps. I <u>know</u> exactly how I did them. Sometimes you hear athletes say they didn't know how they ran so fast or threw so far or jumped that distance. It was just a wonderful accident, a perfect moment coupled with adrenaline.

That's not true for me, at least not anymore. I knew how to do it at USAs and I knew how to do it again at Worlds. I'm going to continue to perfect it, master it, and be able to do it again and again for the rest of my career.

One thing I love about being the first in American history to win a medal is that this will <u>always</u> be mine. Records come and go, but I will always be the first.

Anthem 72

I once was asked the question: "Why are you always telling me thank you." It's true, I find myself saying thank you to him incessantly, for every little thing. Whether he holds the door open, brings me water, or kisses me on the cheek, I respond with gratitude. I express my appreciation when we spend time together. I thank him when he listens attentively and when he shares his thoughts. Saying thank you has become second nature to me.

In general, I have experienced so much gratitude in my life. For every beautiful moment, regardless of its magnitude, I offer my thanks to the Divine. When I do this, a warmth flows through me akin to love. This deepens my gratitude, as I recognize that I am loved enough to have this experience or blessing in the first place. In witnessing a beautiful view, winning a medal, or savoring a delicious meal, I feel love when I express gratitude.

It's the same when I tell people thank you, it conveys more than mere appreciation. It signifies that their actions, their generosity, or simply their presence makes me feel loved. I am grateful for their care, their gestures, and their willingness to be there for me. To me, saying thank you is like saying, "I feel loved."

Anthem 73

I feel like each feather I took was an agreement that I accepted from the divine.

I initially walked past the first feather I found. I saw it, thought it looked interesting, but continued my walk for at least ten steps. Then I stopped, I looked up the meaning and agreed to receive it. I thought of it like God was sending me a business proposal…

"Hey Tori, I have this plan for you. It's pretty amazing. It comes with peace, love, protection, medals, healing, and many other things. BUT I can't just give it to you. You need to be open and willing to receive it. You need to have a certain level of awareness and spiritual openness. Think about it and get back to me."

I picked it up, agreeing to hear more about it. I showed interest. That same day I asked God for another feather, just to see if it would work. Only moments later, there was another feather in my path. It was slightly smaller than the first, but every bit as rich in hue.

This time God said, "I see your interest and openness, so what I'm going to do is give you this feather as a contract. Take it, look it over, keep your mind and heart open, and continue to trust in me throughout the next few weeks. Let stress fall away, let worry disappear, and see how you feel. I'll be in touch."

I took this feather as well. It was that same afternoon that I jumped 18.80 meters in practice. The rest of training had its ups and downs, but I stayed positive. I did not worry. I did not stress. I didn't even get overconfident for jumping 18.80 meters. I remained calm and focused in the week leading up to prelims and finals.

The morning of finals, I found the last beautiful black crow's feather.

God said, "You've done really well these last couple of weeks. I know your mind. I know your heart. And I see that you are ready. I give you this feather as confirmation of our agreement outlined in our previous discussion. By taking this feather it's as if you are signing our agreement. Then the floodgates will open for you. You can move forward fearlessly and with courage. Your mind, body, and spirit are finally in alignment. Go."

I took the feather wrapped it in lavender and grass and placed on top of my uniform.

While on the runway, just before my medal-winning jump, I was reminded that this was already written for me. I completely relaxed. I took my time and jumped 14.72 meters without even touching the board. When I saw the mark go up on the screen, all I could do was nod and laugh a little. God showed me this and it happened. I was amazed but not surprised.

When I ran my victory lap, it all hit me. Flashes of crying in a cardboard bed eating stale cake at the Tokyo Olympics. Images of me leaving the runway in Serbia at the Indoor World Championships with my head hung low. The anxiety of making the decision to move out of the country again to pursue a dream.

I cried with joy. I persevered. I made the decision not to give up on myself. God opened my spirit and showed me the way, lightly guided me on the right path, and I made it.

I did it.

Two days later, my best friend and I went on a mini vacation to the Redwood Forest in Northern California. The massive trees enthralled me and we played in them like children. We climbed trees, jumped off of large mounds of moss and dirt. We stretched our bodies and bent low into cave-like tree stumps. We waded in rivers and smelled the living wood.

Midway through the hike, my best friend and I were literally skipping down the trail, when I was stopped by the most perfectly placed, brilliantly blue feather lodged in a fallen tree. I stared at it with my mouth wide open. It was as if it were waiting for me.

My friend, who'd skipped a few more paces before realizing I'd stopped, walked back towards me spotting the feather as well. His eyes gleamed and he smiled at me. I began reaching for the feather and he gently touched my hand, pausing my motion.

"Let's take this in."

He guided us into a silent meditation of gratitude. We stood beside one another, facing the feather, and closed our eyes. The entire world around us was perfectly still. The wind paused. The birds rested, and there wasn't a hiker in sight. There was only us, this feather, and the gentle warmth of the sun.

In the hush of the forest, I received a message from God.

"Congratulations, Tori. I'm so proud of you. Although this goal has been reached, know that this is only the beginning. We have so much more to do, on the track and otherwise. We will continue to send you signs, just keep your eyes wide, your mind curious, and your heart open. You will always be taken care of and guided."

I smiled, heart so full, and opened my eyes to the magnificent and vibrant forest. The bark shown redder and the leaves greener. The sun shined brighter and the breeze more serene. I plucked the blue feather from the wood and held it carefully in my hands.

I can rest knowing that all the success that will come to me is already written.

Anthem 74

A few weeks ago, I competed in the Monaco diamond league. I went in feeling so confident, free, and alive. Monaco is a beautiful city of winding roads, sea views, and fancy cars. I jumped the best I've ever jumped in my life. Consistent jumps finishing with 14.86m. A new personal best and #2 American All-time mark, just above my #3 All-time mark.

Tonight, is my last competition of the season. I just finished my morning shakeout and I was listening to my normal music but the songs that were playing weren't hitting right. So, I switched to some female led voices. I listened to Warrior by Chloe & Halle then I AM Woman by Emmy Meli.

I remember the first time I really listened to this song. It was amidst my transition to Greece. I was training in the evening by myself at the Easter Michigan University indoor track. Feelings of uncertainty, anxiety, fear, and incompetence clouded my mind. I knew the move was what I needed to do, but I would be lying if I said I didn't have my doubts or reservations.

The workout was repeat 200s and with my mental instability I was on the verge of breaking down. This song not only helped me through a tough workout but it also reminded me of who I am and what I'm capable of. It gave me strength. I ran those tight curves, tears streaming to the lobes of my ears.

I've competed well all season and I feel the opportunity for 'pressure' to set in. I can feel the desire to have and meet expectations. I can feel the push to 'keep performing well.' I feel from other people, from social media, and I'm doing my best to not do it to myself.

Nothing has set in, but I can feel the opportunity for it to. I've mostly been ignoring it. Staying on top of my rituals but today I finally put a face to it. I decided to face it.

I knew I had to put a word on it or it would attempt to disrupt my peace, it would try to make me fearful.

This morning I made sure to be very focused in my affirmations, very intentional in my movement and the same during my morning shakeout. As I listened to the music, I remembered the emotions I'd felt when I first listened and I let the words shower over me, covering me in truth. I relaxed everything and I cried. A deep full flow of tears. I released the pressure, the fear that was trying to creep, and any fear of failure.

"I AM WOMAN. I AM FEARLESS. I AM SEXY. IM DIVINE. IM UNBEATABLE. IM CREATIVE. HONEY YOU CAN GET IN LINE. I AM FEMININE. I AM MASCULINE. I AM ANYTHING I WANT."

I recited. Believing. Knowing.

Then I danced. Freeing myself not only emotionally and spiritually, but physically. Moving. Singing. Spinning. Jumping and winding my hips.

Ain't no pressure on me.
I AM FREE.

Epilogue

I express my gratitude for allowing me to share my thoughts with you and for generously dedicating your time to my words. Your openness to my experiences is deeply appreciated. My sincerest hope is that these pages have evoked emotions within you, sparked curiosity, or inspired you to view things from a different perspective.

I encourage you to confront the fears that confine you, to examine your actions with a critical eye, to nurture loving thoughts that dispel negativity, and to pursue your passions with unwavering enthusiasm. Remember that you are divinely guided and supported, trust your intuition, and know that anything that deeply resonates with you is undoubtedly meant for you.

Embrace the belief that your path is already written, and trust in the unfolding journey.

Thank you once again.
Mee
Tori Franklin

About the Author

Tori Franklin is an esteemed professional triple jumper representing Team USA. Tori made her Olympic debut at the 2021 Tokyo Olympics, marking a significant milestone in her career. In 2022, Tori became the first American woman in history to earn a medal in the triple jump, securing the bronze medal at the IAAF World Championships in Eugene, Oregon. Tori is currently a

4-time USA Champion and is the former indoor and outdoor American record holder in the women's triple jump. She has represented Team USA at the Olympics (2021), four outdoor World Championship meets (2017, 2019, 2022, 2023), and two indoor World Championships (2018, 2022). She is currently ranked #3 in the world.

In addition to her athletic achievements, Tori is a sought-after speaker who travels the country, captivating audiences with her inspiring talks. She also contributes her writing to Medium, sharing her insights and experiences. In addition to her athletic pursuits, Tori continuously expands her knowledge and skillset in many holistic healing practices, currently including reiki, tantra, and therapeutic dance.

Tori pursued her college education at Michigan State University, where she studied interdisciplinary studies with a focus of economics. She set impressive indoor and outdoor records for both MSU and the Big Ten Conference in the triple jump. As well as running the 400m leg for the Big Ten Record in the Distance Medley Relay. Tori went on to earn her MBA from Devry University.

Tori's journey to success, self-confidence, and self-love has not been a straightforward path. Throughout her youth, she grappled with feelings of abandonment, shame, and depression due to experiences of sexual molestation and assault. After a domestic violence incident in college, Tori turned to vlogging as a means of self-healing, bravely sharing her emotions and developing her 'Tori Anthem.' Through affirmations and self-reflection, she gradually overcame negative self-talk and cultivated a profound love for herself.

Now, she is dedicated to sharing her light and positive energy with others. Her aim is to impart valuable lessons on self-love, mental health, and confidence. Tori is thrilled to reach an even wider audience through YOU ANTHEM.